Star Crossed

A Memoir

Star Crossed
A Memoir
by Bette Isacoff

Copyright © 2013 Bette Isacoff

Published by Headwinds Publishing
an imprint of Hard Press Editions
P.O. Box 176, Stockbridge, MA 01262
Director: Anne Bei
Founding Publisher: Jon Gams
Designed by: Jane McWhorter

Printed and bound in China by Regent Publishing Services, Ltd.

Library of Congress Cataloging-in-Publication Data

Isacoff, Bette.
Starcrossed, a memoir / Bette Isacoff.
    pages cm
ISBN-13: 978-0-615-75281-5
ISBN-10: 0-615-75281-0
1. Isacoff, Bette. 2. Interfaith marriage–United States–Biography. I.
Title.
CT275.I67A3 2013
306.84'3092--dc23
[B]
      2013008447

Permissions
Lyrics from "Mrs. Robinson" by Paul Simon. Copyright © 1968 Paul Simon
Used by permission of the Publisher: Paul Simon.

Lyrics from "Time Of The Season" as performed by the Zombies. Copyright © 1968 by Marquis Songs USA—used by permission.

For Richard

Though you were not the man of my dreams,
you've made all my dreams come true.

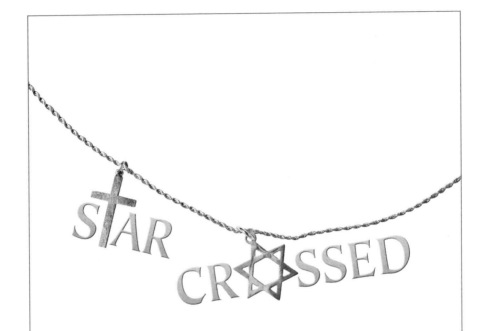

A Memoir

Bette Isacoff

Headwinds Publishing
an imprint of Hard Press Editions
Stockbridge, Massachusetts

Acknowledgements

I am deeply indebted to the late visionary genius, Hard Press Editions Founder and President Jon Gams, who took a fledgling author and a glimmer of a manuscript under his tutelage and turned out a writer and a book. Also to the knowledgeable and capable Director and Managing Editor Anne Bei, who in establishing the Headwinds imprint opened the door for the publication of my book, for her wisdom and guidance. Thank you to the brilliant and inspirational Liz Riviere, Editor and Marketer, who shared my vision for this project, cared about my story as if it were her own, and made *Star Crossed* come to life on the printed page. For her artistic imagination in the initial cover design concept. Perhaps most important, for her constant encouragement and frequent hand-holding.

Thank you also to the innovative and talented Designers, Michelle Quigley and Jane McWhorter. Both of you helped me to produce a stunning book. And to the technically savvy Kit Latham, Online Media Specialist, who manages all sorts of things I don't understand, behind the scenes, on the Internet.

I am grateful to the thoughtful and attentive readers of my first draft: Mariana Bergtold, Julie Bertelli, Pat Holle, Michael Marcus, Danny and Sydney Setzer, Kelly J. Wright, Judy Yvars.

I appreciate the efforts of those who provided photographs from their personal collections: Carol Gondek Fischer, Mindy Isacoff, Stuart Rosenkrantz.

To my college roommate, Carol Gondek Fischer, and our across-the-hall neighbor, Noreen A. Conlon. Thank you for believing in Richard and me when very few did.

Friends and family who gave their unfailing support: Carol Balawender, Henry Bevis, Suzanne Childs, Ethan Dufault, Carol Gondek Fischer, Mary Garrett, Budi Haryanto, Prof. Robert Hubbard, Nancy Hopper, Lynn Murray Kleindeinst, Balinda Lennon, Teresa Mejia, Lynne Turbie Menon, Michael Marcus, Stella Mercier, Belinda Muniak, Rita Norcross, Amy Socia Paloski, Rod Perry, Prof. Charles Rafferty, Stuart and Denise Rosenkrantz, Michael St. John, Judith Scago, Prof. Eric Schoeck, Pat Scully Taddey; Kathy, Mary, Paula, and Victoria; and my daughter Kira. With apologies and gratitude to anyone whom my age-challenged memory may have inadvertently overlooked.

My incredible and exceptional husband, Richard: he is the great love of my life, and I am the great love of his.

Finally I thank God, who took two disparate people on two divergent life paths and brought us, against all odds, together.

In Memoriam

Jonathan (Jon) Gams
1951-2009
President and Publisher, Hard Press Editions

Thank you

Spring 1984

You can't show dogs in your pajamas. We knew that. Just over the Maryland line into Delaware, on our way to a big show weekend on Long Island, we were cruising up Interstate 95 without our clothes. We didn't know *that*. (This is not to imply that we weren't wearing any.) As I turned to answer a question from our five-year-old daughter Kira in the back seat, my mind registered a garment bag hanging in its accustomed place. My eyes saw empty space. Switching gears, my mind took in the scene at home: garment bag draped over the couch, ready to be loaded . . . and still waiting. Sure, we had underwear and sleep wear in the suitcase, but that was it. "RICHARD!" My husband cringed—he knew frantic when he heard it. Only his exceptional skills behind the wheel kept us in our lane.

Jackets and ties were required for men in the show ring; skirts or dresses for the ladies. Our first class would be called promptly at 8:00 a.m., giving us no time to shop in the morning. Lightning quick I remembered, from our many trips up the east coast for dog shows and visits to our families in New England, a huge shopping center which would be looming off to the right any second. "Take the Christiana Mall exit!" I cried. It was eight fifty-three or, more pessimistically, seven minutes before closing time on a Friday night. "They're closing," Richard pointed out the obvious. "They *can't!*" I insisted. He knew better than to argue, and he knew better than to stand in front of a runaway train. He pulled off the highway. "Drop me off, park the car, and meet me inside!" I barked. By now there was a lot of barking going on inside the van.

I jumped out, dragging my bewildered daughter by the hand. We raced through the store entrance faster than a pack of greyhounds charging across the finish line, panting just as hard. Seeking out the most sympathetic-looking clerk, I launched at once into my hard-luck story. "Could you, would you, keep the store open a few extra minutes for us?" A quick consultation with the manager followed. I watched from a short distance away as his eyebrows scrunched together, then flew up to his hairline like fuzzy black caterpillars dangling from skyhooks. Finally a nod and a smile, and the place was ours.

Having been married to me for almost fifteen years, Richard simply shot me his "how did you ever!" look when a men's department sales rep greeted him warmly, making himself available for any assistance my put-upon mate might need. We did our part, shopping in record time, and left with several complete outfits and many, many thanks. Richard, being of unsound mind when it comes to wardrobe size, was aghast at the unnecessary expenditure. He subscribes to the three-is-enough theory: one shirt on his back, one in the laundry, and one in the closet. We girls were delighted at our unanticipated windfall, as too much is never enough when it comes to clothes! We were even able to approximate the style and quality of those we left behind.

I am fond of saying that I have a mind like a steel trap. Richard invariably tacks on, "Once it snaps shut, *nothing* gets in." Still, I am not a slow learner, so you would think I'd have smartened up about leaving clothes behind after a similar fiasco on our wedding night. But no.

FALSE HOPES

Chapter
1

Having selected this particular bowl for its depth, I was sure that the worm would not be able to get away. But the ceramic was rough and grainy, and I watched the creature undulate effortlessly up the side, oozing its way out right under my nose. I snatched it up and held it captive in my hand. I wondered, "What can I do with a worm?" Having heard somewhere that if a worm is cut in half it becomes two live worms, I decided to try it.

Aware that my mother was distracted on the phone, I darted into the kitchen with my specimen and grabbed a sharp knife. Thinking briefly about how it would feel to cut into a steak later with that same knife, I discarded the thought as I would ditch the utensil when I was through with it. I didn't know which end of the slimy, squirmy thing I held between my thumb and forefinger. I sliced slowly, with a sawing motion, through the soft flesh. I held my breath. I watched and waited and could almost sense someone laughing at me. "How could you fall for such a stupid joke? The worm's going to die, dummy!"

But then . . . oh look! They're moving! They're crawling away! An intense feeling of satisfaction came over me. On that day, in my mind, I made the giant leap from kid to doctor.

After three or four tries, I was convinced that the tale was true. I needed to move on. I slouched in the chair and watched two halves of worm try to escape from the bowl. There had to be something else I could do.

Of course! What an idea! Easing the twins into a covered jar for safekeeping, I ran back into the house. I raced upstairs as if the jaws of a croc were snapping at my socks, taking the steps two at a time, my heart a step ahead of me. I bee-lined for my mother's sewing basket. Breathless with excitement, I tested the sharpness of each needle on the tip of a finger and set the best aside. Rummaging through the drawers of her Singer, I found a box of threads. My eyes scanned the rows: what color would she be least likely to use, and therefore probably not miss? I put my money on chartreuse and put my fingers around the spool, palming it into my pocket along with the needle. I flew down the stairs and brought my treasures outside. I would stitch up the two halves of worm!

I laid out my equipment and retrieved the subjects. Immediately, a problem. They wouldn't hold still when I tried to reunite the ends. Another trip inside: this time for pins. I tacked each end down, pinched the two of them together, and began to sew. Biting down hard on my bottom lip, I plunged the needle into living tissue. If it was squishy, icky, or gooey, I didn't notice, so focused was I on what I was doing. The worm segments didn't put up much of a fight. I managed to get in about a half-dozen stitches of various lengths, oddly spaced—some tighter, some looser. To me it was a work of art. Satisfied that the job was done, I carried the patient gingerly to a box lined with tender green leaves and grass, my recovery room. I set him in the sun to keep the little guy warm. Feeling my confidence grow I found more worms, severed and sewed. Into the grassy nest they went.

At dinner I sat fidgeting, dying to tell but smart enough not to. I lay in bed that night knowing, for the very first time, exactly how it felt to be a surgeon. Yes, I was one of them now. I'd operated on a live patient! In the morning I flew outside to check on my charges. Dead. All dead. Every last one of them. Fried, dried, and shriveled to a crisp, along with their bedding. As I sat hunched over my dissecting table, the sun sent out its withering rays, like long straws, and sucked the life right out of them.

Chapter
2

Uncharacteristically, for I was not a difficult child, I demanded a doctor kit. I was hugely disappointed when I got a toy version and not the real thing. I subjected everyone who would cooperate to bizarre physical examinations and related tortures. They tolerated the thermometers and jerked their knees obligingly for the reflex hammer, but drew a firm line at anything involving even plastic needles, scalpels, or scissors. Positioning a stethoscope carefully in my ears, I placed the bell on a body part, listened intently, and nodded in satisfaction as I heard . . . absolutely nothing. I was frustrated by the limits of make-believe. Then, fate intervened and—for real!—I had to go to the hospital.

In the early fifties, children routinely had tonsillectomies. At the age of seven, sitting in my pediatrician's office, I heard the words that caused my soul to sing: "I'm afraid they'll have to come out." He tried to be kind, to soften the blow, but I was barely listening. *I was going to have an operation!* I could hardly contain my excitement. In the days that followed I danced around the neighborhood, sharing the great news with anyone I could find. Why was I getting funny looks?

I was placed in a four-bed ward with private duty nurses around the clock, more for my mother's peace of mind than for me. Walking with my caretaker through the halls prior to surgery, I felt as though I'd finally come home. I had no fear or anxiety and went willingly, even eagerly, to the operating room. I was in heaven! As they placed the cone over my nose I fought the drug, trying my best to see every single thing in this enchanted place. Then, oblivion.

When I recovered from the ether anesthetic, I discovered a new source of ecstasy right across the room. From my crib I stared nonstop at the only patient in the ward who was seriously ill. Curious George I was, in typical monkey pose—little paws curled around the bars and nose thrust between. I was riveted by the tubes, lines, and drains attached to and snaking from his frail body. There was an extra pair of eyes and an additional set of hands at each of his treatments, if only in my imagination. When a doctor got in the way and blocked my view I was furious, and craned this way and that to see around him. I wanted badly to be doing what the doctors did. I paid the nurses no mind, as bedpans and blood pressure cuffs held no interest whatsoever for me. Little boy, whoever you are, wherever you are, please forgive me. I was nosy and rude, filled with morbid curiosity; I absolutely could not help myself.

Once I was discharged, I wracked my brain for ways to practice medicine. The answer finally came to me: I actually did have patients at my disposal! Across the street from our home was a wooded area covering many acres. I gathered up as many emergency supplies as I could find or fashion and prepared a first aid kit. Stashed in the forest, it would be available to me for the care of sick or injured animals. I spent as much time there as I possibly could and managed to minister to a fair share of Nature's less fortunate critters.

Engrossed in my work, in love with my life, I frequently lost track of time as I was totally and completely focused on my clinical skills. My mother would call me home for dinner, yelling until she was hoarse. Eventually she took to using a green plastic whistle in the shape of a locomotive, with a sound every bit as loud. Though I developed selective deafness, sooner or later I would return to the house to reenergize for morning. Each night I fell asleep picturing the rescues I would orchestrate the next day. I didn't exactly set traps to ensnare hapless squirrels and bunnies so I could splint their broken legs, but if one so impaired happened along I was eager to put my abilities to the test. Feeling great empathy for the frightened little sufferer, I would gently lift it from its resting place, cradling it reassuringly as I assessed the damage. Having always felt a strong kinship with animals, I sensed a special closeness to those in misery. Throughout the examination and treatment I whispered, sang quietly, or murmured encouragement. I sustained them during the procedures and nurtured them in the recovery phase.

Then came the summer of my advanced experimentation, when I ventured next door.

Chapter
3

Our neighbors had a lovely, multi-tiered estate which included three reflecting pools of different sizes and shapes. One, an oval, was home to several koi—large goldfish. Each little pond resonated with croaks and twangs that harmonized with the chirps of insects, creating a symphony to enhance the romance of a summer's night. But it was science, not art, that was on my mind. It gradually dawned on me that I had a ready source of vertebrates for my homemade scalpel—frogs! *It may have been the frogs that derailed my career in medicine.*

Because wife and children summered in Connecticut, and the man of the house joined them on weekends, I would have ample time to sneak in, steal a frog or two, and slink back home without being detected. Something told me that I shouldn't; that it was wrong. I knew my parents would kill me if they ever found out. On the other hand, how could I resist? The frogs were right there! Practically begging to be taken. Even as I agonized over my choices, I knew what I was going to do. The urge was too strong; the temptation too great. As the homeowner was himself a physician, I chose to believe that he wouldn't mind, and might even be impressed by my ingenuity! I convinced myself that he would probably be pleased to be making a significant contribution to my medical education. In preparation, I constructed a holding pen consisting of a little bricked area with smaller wading bowl, and a screen over the top to prevent escape. My laboratory was ready. The patio would be my operating room.

But when the time actually came to do the deed, my bravado deserted me. I guessed that the good doctor would not be at all supportive of my forays into his lavishly landscaped showplace, and my guess is that I guessed right. However my initial fear of being discovered, "*What was that? A car door slammed! . . . Okay, false alarm,*" quickly gave way to exhilaration at the prospect of snagging some live specimens for my experiments.

I already knew what I planned to do with them. I had discovered a Sunday-morning television show, *The Seekers,* which featured a real surgical procedure each week. Though I watched it religiously, black-and-white TV did not do justice to blood red, gall bladder green, liver brown, and lung pink. Now I would see what those doctors saw and operate just like they did.

Shaking in anticipation of doing more sophisticated surgery than the worms allowed, I slipped through the tall shrubbery that divided our properties. Fleet of feet I scurried, on tippy-toe, across the vast expanse of lush, green lawn. My steps were light as air, my heart a leaden basketball ricocheting off my ribs. I could feel its pounding in my ears.

As I inched closer I spotted my prey, plump and placid, lounging on lily pads. I covered the remaining distance prone, a wily serpent in my own personal Garden of Eden. But they were onto me and dove for safety. I was smarter, and I had a plan. I hovered at the water's edge, and soon enough a couple of frogs surfaced at the rim of the pool. We were nose-to-nose. "Come here, little froggy," I hissed. The frog stared back, unwilling to cooperate. Mosquitoes skimming the surface of the water dropped to their knees for a prayer of thanksgiving and a quick grace-before-meals as I thrust my succulent arm in their direction. Stealthily I eased my hand forward until I was able to grasp the croaker around its midsection. I did not blanch at the slimy vegetation through which I plunged my arm or the various bugs that danced on my skin. My fingers closed, gently but firmly, around the object of my desire. I had a living, breathing, laboratory animal! Euphoria carried me and my prize home.

I went back, again and again, for more. As befitting their classy surroundings the mosquitoes, obviously high-bred and well-versed in manners and etiquette, left their calling cards as any proper socialite would.

How did I feel as I set up my first subject for study? Don't even ask how I reconciled my great love of all things furred and feathered with a swift, cold slice into tender frog flesh! I felt fine, and it felt right. Emboldened by my quest for the greater good, I was able to offer up these amphibians on the altar of medical research without a qualm. At last I'd be on the inside looking in, in glorious, three-dimensional, living color. A whole new world was literally at my fingertips, provided I didn't slip and sever them. I was ready to embrace it. No meek, halfhearted nick of the skin for me. I carved open the belly from neck to nether regions in one strong stroke.

What treasures awaited me within! Real muscles; honest-to-goodness bones. Poking and prodding, I sternly quizzed myself on the various structures I found (mostly, I had no idea what I was looking at). It was enough just to be there—to have an instrument in my hand and blood on my clothes. A contentment and satisfaction that I never anticipated washed over me. A passion to defeat disease, and triumph in the face of trauma, engulfed me. This was where I belonged; this was what I was destined to do. I could almost feel the weight of a stethoscope on my shoulders. Over the next several weeks I developed and refined my mastery, longing for the day when I would be admitted to high school, there to study my favorite subject, biology.

Up to this point, all was well. My parents, assuming I was keeping the frogs as pets and not knowing from whence they came, looked the other way—Dad in amusement, Mom in disgust. Were it not for the Labor Day barbecue, I might be a trauma surgeon today. If only I had been the one to lay the dinner mats on the patio table, which now held the sun-dried remains of frog guts! Instead, my mother emerged with the place settings like she'd just stepped out of the pages of a *Better Homes and Gardens* "End-of-Summer Celebrations" article. She startled, as if an electric current had sizzled through the serving tray, and ran screaming into the house before the linen could caress the glass. Storming out, my father—all six feet, two-and-a-half inches of him—nearly carved me up with my own dissecting instrument for contaminating and ruining this expensive piece of furniture. The full impact of what I had been doing finally hit him, and he had to restrain himself from hitting me! Not that he ever would, really, but it was a long time before I proposed the idea of medical school again.

This is not to say, however, that I abandoned my pursuits. I had an older cousin, a sure shot and a good sport, with a similar interest in becoming a doctor. Together, we began to knock squirrels out of trees. I was the spotter, and he took aim and fired with minimal damage to the carcass which would later be placed on display. We peeled back the pelt and gutted the rodent. I recall soaking cotton balls in a solution of borax; they would replace the innards. When the squirrel was stuffed, stitched, and reshaped to our satisfaction, we mounted it on a small log. Admiring our trophy, we congratulated each other for a job well done.

While not exactly a healing science, taxidermy enabled us to mimic our heroes in yet another way, and I graduated from amphibians to mammals. We practiced our craft in his garage. Whenever my mother called outside to tell me it was time to leave, I'd beg for a few more minutes. When she asked what we were doing, I simply said, "Stuffing squirrels." She thought we were over-feeding them. I let her believe it.

Chapter
4

Finally, a dream come true! I entered my sophomore year of high school and headed straight for the biology lab. Even before the course formally started I would visit whenever I could, inspecting the instruments and microscopes with anticipation and awe. Impatiently I suffered through the amoebae and protozoa, anxious for more meaty stuff that I could sink my teeth into. At last, the frogs.

Was I ever in for a surprise! To my dismay and utter amazement, I learned that experimental subjects are supposed to be dead *before* they are dissected. A merciful procedure known as pithing, whereby the spinal cord is swiftly severed, was supposedly painless. I never got an opinion from the frog, but this method had to be less traumatic than the slow, torturous deaths my earlier victims suffered at my hands. I was wracked with guilt over the devastation I had wrought on these innocents for my own selfish reasons. Though I could not atone for my earlier cruelty, I vowed to be the best surgeon possible, so that they would not have suffered in vain. I rededicated myself to my studies with a new, stronger sense of purpose.

Meanwhile, at home, my parents were dropping not-so-subtle hints about my future. "So-and-so has become a teacher. Isn't that wonderful?" "Such-and-such a nursing school is supposed to be the best in the area." At that time, in my family, a college education was about insurance, not a career. In all probability, I would only work until I found a man to work *for* me. "If something should happen to your husband, you could always fall back on . . . ." I knew where this was going. My dreams were amusing, even cute and clever, but reality would be ruled by practicality. My list of eventual job possibilities was being whittled down to two, with teaching preferred over nursing as it meant a college degree as opposed to a diploma. I had already rejected nursing outright. Nothing less than doctor would do. Eventually there came a point at which a serious discussion of my college major was unavoidable, as I wrestled with a homework assignment to complete a sample admission form. I mustered my courage and approached my father with the paper.

Chapter
5

Smoke, drink, swear, have sex, act unladylike in public—these were all things I dared not do, because of my father. Well, not because of my *father*, but because of my *mother* because of my father. He was a hero to many people, but my mother made him a saint to me. Often I heard variations of "It's all right for (Mary, Judy, Susan) to behave that way. Her father is a (fill in a trade). Your father is in the public eye all the time. You must never do anything that would reflect badly on him."

My father, Tullio A. Francesconi, came with his family to America when he was fourteen. As a young boy in northern Italy, he would sit at the window and gaze longingly at the Fascist Blackshirt youth on the march past his house. Knowing nothing of their ideology, he begged his father to let him join. My grandfather, having less than no use for the evil dictator, all but smacked his misguided son across the room. The lad would not be joining the troops. But soon enough Mussolini would figure prominently in his life.

My father's grandmother and Benito Mussolini's mother were sisters, which made my grandmother and Mussolini first cousins. In fact my grandmother, Rosa, was named after Mussolini's mother (her aunt)—also Rosa. When things started to go bad in Italy, the natives began to leave in droves. To stem the tide, Mussolini declared a moratorium on emigration. My grandparents decided to flee with the family to America, but they had difficulty getting out. When all other avenues failed, my grandmother put in a call to her cousin. She asked that Mussolini allow them passage on the last boat that would leave the country with Italians bound for the United States. Outraged, he refused, but she argued persuasively. Finally she wore him down, and they were granted permission and a place on the ship. And so they came to Massachusetts. Benito would reach his long arm out across the Atlantic later, when a draft notice arrived in the mail for my father to fulfill his obligation to the Italian army. Tossing it into the trash, the young man gave it no further thought.

Having completed high school in Europe, Dad enrolled in grammar school here to learn English. He repeated high school as well, graduating with highest honors. He was also Student Council president and a letter athlete in football, basketball, and track and field. Tall and exceedingly handsome, with light skin and blue eyes, he spoke without a trace of an accent and without the hand gestures commonly attributed to persons of his ethnic background. He considered himself an American of Italian ancestry. By the time I came along he was a successful attorney, but not just any attorney. Scrapbooks with clippings from newspaper articles in which he is featured are filled to overflowing.

My father was highly regarded in many different circles. Active in the Republican Party, he was friends with Dwight Eisenhower, Leverett Saltonstall, Henry Cabot Lodge, Elliott Richardson, Bruce Crane (of the prominent paper manufacturing company whose product, imprinted with photos of presidents and statesmen, we regularly exchange for various goods and services), and several Massachusetts governors and other notables. I got to meet many of them too, as I accompanied him to fundraisers and other party functions at which high-profile stars would entertain. Curiously, he was well-thought-of by Democrats as well, and was asked by Larry O'Brien to run John Kennedy's presidential campaign in Western Massachusetts. He declined.

Having grown up in the south end of Springfield, an area of apartment buildings and three-story homes populated by Italian immigrant families, he regularly played with kids who later became members of organized crime, but he chose a different path. A man of great integrity and principle, he was respected by the criminal element. On one occasion when he was Chairman of the Police Commission, he was approached by them regarding the promotion of a certain individual to the rank of sergeant. The man was not as qualified as some other applicants and therefore not a serious contender for the position. My father stood his ground, and those called back for repeat interviews did not include their candidate.

Suddenly, without knowing why, I was told to come straight home after school every day. I could not participate in extracurricular activities, nor could I visit friends. No explanation was given, but I could sense a tension in the house that was not there before. In time I would learn that, although the bosses did not dare cross my father, some underling trying to flex his muscle had threatened our family. Eventually the job was given to the man best-suited, and the upstart was not heard from again. A little footnote: when a certain one of the "guys" read my engagement announcement in the paper years later he called my father, offering the services of Frank Sinatra to sing at my wedding! Never having accepted a favor from that group, my dad was not about to start then, and I was just as glad. Sinatra was not my taste in music.

Apparently Dad's accomplishments did not escape the notice of the Italian Ambassador to the United States, who called one day to report that my father was to be knighted by the Republic of Italy with the rank of Cavaliere. A formal dinner was planned, at which Dad would receive the *Stella della Solidarietà Italiana*—the Star of Italian Solidarity. Honored though he was, a little worry niggle gnawed at his conscience. He began to wonder: at the ceremony would he be handed an award, or the Italian equivalent of an arrest warrant? Remember those army draft papers he discarded? He was a deserter! Did they know? Would they find out? Did they care? But that night they gave him only accolades, an impressive medal and lapel rosette (he never wore either), and a certificate signed by the country's president.

However when the local UNICO (an Italian-American service organization whose name means "unique"—an acronym for Unity, Neighborliness, Integrity, Charity, and Opportunity) chapter wanted to fete him for being Springfield's first Italian judge he declined the tribute, making it clear that he was not an *Italian* judge. He felt that he could not assure impartiality on the bench were he to be so designated. He was, he said, a judge for all the people.

As a child, of course, I did not know any of this. This hero, this saint, was just daddy to me, and I was definitely his little girl. I remember the great hurricane of 1955, when damage was extensive and roads were washed away. We had a date to see the circus that afternoon. Despite pleas from my mother to stay home my father took me, by out-of-the-way roads and imaginative detours, to the show. I had the time of my life. I also recall a Kingston Trio concert, where I was desperate to snag an autograph. My dad stretched his long frame over the crowd and handed them a scrap of paper—I have it still. I appreciated his willingness to wangle me in to see Pop Singer at his famous drug store next to the studio where *American Bandstand* was telecast. I even got to sit with some of the regulars from the show for a soda, while he and the proprietor chatted away like old friends. This was the only time in my entire life that I am aware of his ever pulling rank, for any reason whatsoever, as he was basically a very humble man.

Oh, but he could give off an air of arrogance when the occasion demanded. One night my parents took me to the ice rink, where our figure skating club was having its annual Halloween party. Everyone was urged to come in costume. For weeks members were asking, "Tullio, what are you going to wear?" Annoyed, he would growl, "I am not dressing up."

That evening he walked into the arena in street clothes, snapping impatiently at anyone who remarked about his refusal to participate in the festivities. The obvious implication was that he was above such frivolity. We skated the first half of the session—Dad enjoyed the sport too, and was on the ice with me—when intermission was called so the Zamboni could resurface. As we returned to the ice for costume judging, everyone's attention was drawn to Little Lord Fauntleroy: a very tall man in black shorts, bolero, and knee socks; a white shirt with Peter Pan collar; huge purple satin bow at the neck; and a white sailor hat with long streamers down the back. He had a Little Lulu wig on his head and a swirly-colored all-day sucker in his hand. Because he was not a strong skater, he had a natural hesitancy that was right in character. People took mental inventory, whispering among themselves, until they eliminated everyone it could possibly be. Then it dawned on them: it was my father. The place erupted! They howled, they screamed, they stamped, they cheered. They awarded him first prize. And they loved him.

Chapter
6

Like most children in the fifties, I had two parents at home. Unlike most kids, I had a father and a *smother*. My maternal grandmother, Mary Krupa, died suddenly at the age of forty, leaving my eighteen-year-old mother Veronica to look after six younger siblings. In order to deal with her own grief, the trauma to her family, and the rigors of raising a newly-motherless brood, she developed rigid coping mechanisms including obsessive attention to detail, a high degree of control, and excessive vigilance. Keenly aware of the impact of their mother's loss on the children, she vowed that when she had her own they would never know hardship; never struggle; never want for anything.

Because of the intervention of World War II, Mom did not start her family until she was thirty-seven, and I was that later-in-life baby and her only child. Used to ministering to many, she now focused all of her limitless energy on me. She doted; she catered; she served. Having given over her late teens and early twenties to the care of her brothers and sisters, she developed no life of her own. She overcompensated for this loss by living vicariously through my father and me. She had a personal stake in our successes and suffered our setbacks as though they were her own.

In order to spare me the pain of failure, she orchestrated my life down to the minute. She also simplified it. I had only two concerns: the right thing and the best way. I needed to "do the right thing" in public, so that people would approve of me and compliment her for raising such a fine daughter; and I needed to conduct my daily affairs "the best way," meaning her way, to spare me undue effort and exertion. She released me from the obligation to think for myself, thereby protecting me from making a wrong move.

I had no responsibilities except piano practice, but I was expected to do that religiously. It didn't matter that I did not for one minute want to play the piano. I was taken to an aunt for haircuts so as not to offend a family member, even though her hairdressing skills were more suited to her usual clientele of much older women. As a result in high school, when the other girls had swinging hair and bangs, I had a pompadour. It did nothing for my looks or my popularity. If my mother sneezed, I was confined to bed for a day or two, just to be safe. If she was cold, I was handed a sweater.

Ah yes, the sweater—the butt of countless family jokes. When I was teased about it, I did not realize that people were chuckling about my mother's overprotectiveness. I assumed they were making fun of me. The sweater thing came to a head when I was seventeen, on a sweltering August day that was hotter than the freshly-stoked fires of hell. I was going to a local park to play tennis with a friend, and would meet her at her house. As I was slipping out the door my mother called after me, "Take your sweater!" I stepped back inside and slammed the door behind me. "I will not take a sweater on the hottest day of the year. I'll look like a jerk! No one else will have a sweater." She had an answer ready: "Of course it's the hottest day of the year. That's why you need the sweater. When you're through playing you'll be all perspired, and you'll catch a cold if you don't cover up. Take the sweater." "NO!" I dared to refuse. "Yes!" she countered. I appealed to the voice of reason, my father. "Daaad!" I began, but he was unmoved. "Take your sweater," he said flatly.

I was stunned. I was used to a certain amount of unreasonableness from my mother and I fully recognized that, while it could be a nuisance, she was doing it solely out of love and concern for me. But I truly expected my father to know better and to do better. He disappointed me that day. I grabbed the pullover, stormed out of the house, and headed to my friend's place where I stashed the thing, stopping by on the way back home to pick it up. They of course didn't know, and I assumed that that was the end of the episode.

A few years later, home from college for the summer, I was visiting an aunt with my mother. The two women were sitting out on the deck, watching my younger cousins frolic in the pool. My old squirrel-stuffing partner and I were underneath the structure, looking for rhubarb. I picked up snatches of a conversation that caused my ears to prick and rotate in the direction of the remarks. "I insisted that she bring a sweater," I heard, "and she said 'no.' But he made her take it. As soon as she was gone, though, he let me have it. 'Don't you ever, ever, do that to her again! She is old enough to decide if she needs a sweater. If she gets sick this time, she'll take one next time! But you have to stop hovering like this.'" I froze in my tracks. Dad had come through after all! Long before psychology was popular, he was aware of the importance of parents presenting a united front to their children, but he had taken my mother to task later, in private. I felt a whole lot better knowing that I had my dad's silent support. Though I did not always agree with him, I knew that he tried to be fair. This time he did things the right way.

Had he taken as firm a stand on the issue of naming his only child, my life might have been much simpler. With a surname like Francesconi, you'd think that the need for a short first name would be obvious. My mother explained how she came up with Elizabeth: growing up Polish in a small, predominantly Polish town, she was intrigued by a local society girl named Elizabeth Fitzgerald. Of course you have figured out that "society" here is relative, but there it was: I was named Elizabeth Francesconi. What a mouthful! Mom thought it was distinctive. To me it was cumbersome and unflattering, especially among peers with perky names like Lynn Murray and Susan Hartley. It even had a certain cadence—eLIZabeth FRANcesCOni—that, though I was tall and thin, made me feel like a lumbering polar bear in a field of sleek, agile wolves. My self-image, already bruised by this massive moniker, suffered death throes from the other thing about me that was too big: my nose. Bumpy and turned slightly under, it poked out defiantly from my long, narrow face, attracting stares like metal to a magnet. Along with my dumpy hairstyle, my lumpy nose made me feel unattractive, and I was. It seemed that nature had dealt me a nasty blow that even my all-powerful dad could not fix.

While my name was well-intended, my nose an accident of nature, and my hairstyle nothing more than an attempt to flatter her brother's wife, my mother made one crucial, purposeful mistake that cost me dearly for much of my life. She was quick and persistent in pointing out to me my flaws and failings, but steadfastly refused to compliment or acknowledge any of my good points (there had to be some). Sure, she often compared one of my dresses favorably to another little girl's, but she'd made it. She noted how much better my thick, long hair looked than the messy braids on another child, but she'd curled it. When it was about her, the praise was free-flowing. But the mirror she held up to me reflected back an ungainly, awkward, homely kid. After I reached adulthood, I asked her why she'd been so critical of me in my youth. She had a simple answer, rooted securely in the culture of the fifties. "I didn't want you to be conceited," she explained. Now almost obsolete, that adjective struck a mighty blow to the status and popularity of youngsters at the time. There was no crueler epithet, no greater insult. The damage she did in the name of love and concern was significant.

Chapter
7

When my father was right, he was right. And no one was righter than he. In fact this was usually true, as many people who would disagree with him learned over the years. His arguments were well-reasoned and his statements were difficult, if not impossible, to contradict. This is what I faced as I dared approach my father, at the beginning of 1963, with my sample college application. The brave, daring adventurer who patched up animals, sliced into frog bellies, and scooped out squirrel insides trembled at the thought of the task at hand. Special though our relationship was, I was in absolute awe of this man and I already knew his thinking on the matter. I wondered how best to bring up the subject. In the back of my mind were those bits and pieces of frog on the patio table—would he remember? Would he hold that against me? I paced outside the door, rehearsing several scenarios in my mind. At this time, in this place, I was terrified of him.

How would I open the conversation? Confidently? "Hey Dad, since I'm going to be a doctor, I guess I'll major in biology, huh?" Or in supplication? "Please Dad, I really, really want to be a doctor, okay?" In the end, I entered the room where he sat reading, burst into tears, and wailed, "*I want to be a doctor!*" Wordlessly I pointed to a line: Prospective Major_____. He sighed and invited me to join him, and gave me the advice that would change the direction of my life. "If it's what you want," he said, "I'll put you through medical school. But I suggest that you go into teaching instead . . . ." The tears flowed freely, and my bottom lip quivered as he went on. "If something should happen to your husband, you could always fall back on . . . ." *Where had I heard that before? A woman didn't need a career; she needed insurance.* But I needed to be a doctor! I whined, I pleaded, to no avail. His words wafted past me unheeded, but his tone told me everything I needed to know: there would be no medical school for me. His offer had been merely rhetorical. I crumbled in on myself as I sensed my vision fading into nothingness.

I'd expected that he might say no to medical school because of the trouble my interest in medicine had caused at that Labor Day barbecue. All the while, though, as I spoke, he was not thinking about that at all. His mind was going in a completely different direction—the practicality of teaching for a woman. It was not about the frogs after all. Here I'd worried all this time and justifiably so, but for the wrong reason.

This was the early sixties, when women doctors were relatively rare. He was anticipating the difficulties I would surely have in this male bastion, and wanted to spare me grief and heartache. I was willing to endure whatever I encountered in order to earn my MD degree, but I was unable to defy my father. For all that I looked just like him, acted much like him, and certainly had his sense of humor, we differed in one significant way: I was as passionate as he was practical. Where I was enthralled by the drama, the cliff-hanging life-and-death scenarios that were medicine, he focused on the sensible way to a stable future. And this time, in his mind, no one was righter than he— least of all me. His words were more command than counsel: you will be a teacher.

Inside I screamed and raged against this destroyer of my vision, but all I could do was swipe my nose across my sleeve and slink away in defeat. The man that I loved more than anyone else in the world had just slammed the door on the gateway to the rest of my life. I did not understand, then, that he truly did not understand. He was trying to do his best for me. I felt myself shriveling inside as my worms had in that scorching sun; pinioned as my frogs tacked to the table. The stuffing, the stuff of which I was made, my *life*, was being squeezed out of me. Suddenly I was very, very small. My courage, my optimism, my belief in myself were gone.

I had never entertained even the remotest possibility of another career. Yet here I was, one year later, closing in on high school graduation with no direction. I'd been thrust toward the classroom. But what subject would I teach? Not biology, certainly—if I couldn't go all the way with it, I would not go anywhere at all. Having no interest in any particular field, I decided on English. I could read, and I could write. Devastated, I entered "English" as my intended major on that line and kissed my plans goodbye. Scrubs and gloves, clamps and sutures—the objects of my fantasy for as long as I could remember—would be replaced by neat little suits, erasers, and rulers. My passion died, and with it my dream of a future in medicine.

Meanwhile, I was not yet at college and was still very much under mom's weighty thumb. By now I had learned to speak and act according to her dictates. Sometimes she even spoke for me, to keep me from saying the wrong thing. I recall an instance when an acquaintance we hadn't seen for some time stopped to chat. "How do you like the piano?" she asked me. Quickly my mom jumped in with a reply: "She loves it!" In fact, I hated it and would have given anything to quit, but she wouldn't hear of it. "Imagine some day at Christmastime, when you're at a party and everyone is gathered around the piano to sing. You'll be the one playing the piano!" *Yeah,* I thought to myself, *just imagine.* I was flirting with the electric-guitar-fueled swinging sixties; she was stuck in a tickle-the-ivories forties reverie.

When I occasionally managed to blurt out an answer before she had the chance to edit, it became her mission to save face at my expense. My opinion was not respected; it was often ridiculed, then corrected. Through gritted teeth she'd say to me, "Of course you enjoy the piano!" Then, to her audience, with a look of pained tolerance: "She just says she doesn't like to play because her cousin tells her he doesn't." I learned that I had no right to my thoughts; that they weren't valid if they conflicted with hers. It would be many years before I realized that my mother saw me as an extension of herself and not a unique individual.

Ultimately, the piano issue would resolve itself. "Be careful what you ask for . . . ." In the summer of my thirteenth year, I sat on a canvas folding chair's wooden footrest, which collapsed beneath me. As I grabbed the frame, it closed on two fingers of my left hand. I fell directly on top of it, severing the tip of one. Though it was surgically reattached, my playing days were over. My wound would eventually heal, but I would be rid of that dreaded instrument forever! And mom couldn't do a thing about it.

Given few choices, I wrapped myself in a cloak of conformity and behaved as I was instructed. But if I didn't have options, at least some dreams survived. I pictured myself arched gracefully over a silver blade, tracing precise figure eights into clean, hard ice. In my fantasies I drove a dog team of eager Siberians across the frozen tundra. I craved the simple life my schoolmates and neighborhood friends seemed to have. These kids were allowed to make mistakes and learn from them. Though I begged for chores—the next-door-neighbors' children would earn twenty-five cents per bushel of weeds they picked—I was refused. There went a fine opportunity for me to gain some self-esteem, pride of achievement, and a sense of responsibility. Instead of thinking for myself, I always looked to my parents for instruction as I had been taught. They encouraged my dependence rather than helping me to mature.

More often than they knew, I peeked out from the safety of my conformity cocoon and even, on occasion, dared to defy them. One day, my friend and I decided to try smoking for the first time. We were about twelve years old, too young by far to purchase cigarettes. I recalled a small sample pack which sat on top of our refrigerator, left over from the days when my father was a smoker and standing by should he ever feel the urgent need to light up. As he had kicked the habit some years before, I did not think they would be missed. When no one was looking I snatched them, and the next day Lynn and I went into the woods—I with the cigarettes, she with matches. We lit up and roughly approximated smoking behavior; then we went home, unimpressed. A few hours later I was sicker than I'd ever been before. Barely grazing my lungs, the smoke went full-force after my stomach, which erupted like a fire hydrant opened by inner-city kids on a steamy summer day. I did not make the connection, but evidently my parents did. The following night, at dinner, my father casually asked my mother if she had ever removed the cigarettes from above the fridge, as he was sure he'd have no use for them and besides, they were so old now that they'd probably kill anyone who smoked them! He didn't need to say any more, and I never smoked again. I learned that there was no going up against him. He would outmaneuver me, no matter what.

After my mother fell for some story—okay, it might have been true—about Smith College girls sunbathing nude on the roof of their dorm as nearby Westover AFB pilots flew overhead (yeah, like they could buzz low enough to see anything exciting in a B-52 . . . but hey, binoculars?), my parents narrowed my college choices to a few Catholic schools for women. I had scant interest and no preference. Overheard in conversation, a chance comment about The Whale, an ice rink on the campus of Yale University, led me to choose Albertus Magnus College in New Haven. This building, shaped like—what else?—was within walking distance of the Albertus campus. There I could pursue my other passion, figure skating. The ability to indulge my love of and devotion to skating would compensate in some small way for the blow my father had dealt me.

But how could I sustain my disappointment when he agreed to a special high school graduation present? I had an after-school job from which he would pick me up at dinnertime. One day, sitting in the front seat of the car, I reached behind him for his briefcase and took out the newspaper. Grasping the weighty bag by the handle I tossed it back over my shoulder, clipping my nose with the corner. Never believing it could possibly be any bigger, I watched in horror as it swelled and discolored. The next day, dad dropped my mother and me at the doctor's office so the damage could be assessed. A quick exam showed a crack across the bridge that would repair itself, but the plastic surgeon was not through with me. Gripping my chin firmly in hand, he turned my face this way and that, with more than a few drawn-out "hmmm" sounds. Delicately, he suggested that perhaps I might want to do something about my nose? *Would I?????* I went to work on my mother right there in the office. The doc pulled out a photo album of befores-and-afters for us to study, and I was hooked. So was my nose, of course, which was the whole point of this exercise. Typically, my mother would not make such a momentous decision by herself. I got the standard "We'll have to ask Dad" response. From the time he picked us up I was non-stop talk and, being a true attorney's daughter, I presented a strong and persuasive argument.

Many girls anticipated expensive wristwatches, the standard gift. I would have a nose job! Since it was cosmetic surgery insurance would not pay, but Dad came through. Four days after commencement I entered the hospital with high hopes for a low profile. My wish came true as the skilled plastic surgeon cut and carved, leaving me with a sassy new snout. My roommate was a thirteen-year-old girl who had endured months of scorn and stares as her belly grew and grew. Throughout, she insisted that she never had sex. She never did. What she did have was an eleven-pound tumor, successfully removed in a lengthy and dangerous operation. Together we roamed the halls, I with my bandaged face from an elective procedure and she, abdominal dressing hidden beneath her hospital gown, looking healthy as could be. Because the whites of my eyes were solid red and the swollen flesh around them stained in rainbow hues of blue, purple, green, and yellow, I looked pathetic and garnered all of the attention and sympathy from staff and people passing by. This young girl, who had suffered so much, got nary a glance.

Little hospital urchins, we floated through the halls like hobgoblins cruising the neighborhood on Halloween night. While she was happy just to tag along, I was on a mission: I had to find the morgue. This morbid curiosity was a natural result of my interest in how the human body worked, and I wanted to see what happened when it didn't. Thinking I would conquer the last frontier when I opened that cold storage door, I dragged my companion down hallways and up staircases. Every other department was labeled: pharmacy, chapel, x-ray, lab. Morgues, I have since learned, are incognito. No employee would show us the way. The dead would keep their secrets to themselves.

Several days after my discharge from the hospital, I was surprised to receive in the mail an official-looking document from Probate Court. What could they possibly want with me? Once again, Dad worked his magic: he had my name legally shortened from Elizabeth to Bette. Without the weight of my old name and nose, my spirit lightened and began to soar. I couldn't wait to try out my new self at college!

Chapter
8

In September of 1964 I went off to New Haven, Connecticut, with the goal of becoming a high school English teacher. My parents did not push me from the nest, so that I might learn to fly on my own. They hand-delivered me to another nest: an all-female environment, run by nuns, with house-mothers and curfews. My new digs? The only modern dormitory on a lovely campus of stately older mansions. My mother was thrilled because it was new and clean. I was disappointed at its plain functionality. As soon as we walked in the door, I knew I was different from the rest of the freshmen. I had on a dress, with stockings and heels; my parents wore suits. We tried to make overtures of friendship, and people were nice to us, but I was sure the girls could see what I could feel: we weren't like the others. We were so standoffish, formal and reserved, treating this like a state occasion. The other students and their families, in slacks and sweaters, were relaxed and free-spirited. Later that night, in an attempt to loosen me up a little, my dorm-mates short-sheeted my bed. Never having been to summer camp I was not wise to this stunt, and my total confusion amused them more than the deed itself. It really emphasized how sheltered and naïve I was.

After a quick dinner in town, my parents dropped me off at school and started back to Springfield. Climbing the stairs to my floor, I stood in the middle of the lounge and watched, completely bewildered at the activity around me, as the freshmen got to know each other. I saw how they walked up to total strangers and introduced themselves; how they knew what to say and what to do. I was lost. My assigned roommate, Diane, had come equipped with an existing circle of friends. She was one of several students from nearby towns who could have commuted, but elected instead to live on campus. I looked elsewhere for that one girl who would be my exclusive friend, to perpetuate the type of relationship encouraged by my mother throughout my childhood. It was all I knew. To my dismay, no one was interested in foregoing the excitement of meeting new people and forging new friendships to babysit for me. I studied the girls as they jockeyed for position in the pack, and the leaders emerged right away. The others soon fell into line based on personality, looks, and smarts. I didn't fall in at all—I just didn't fit anywhere. I was lonely and homesick, and I'd only been there a few hours!

Can you understand me if I say that I was homesick and thrilled to be away from home at the same time? That very night an older student cut off my long hair and gave me a short, updated style. My mother wasn't there to object! I went where I pleased and wore what I wanted without interference! I tasted freedom for the very first time. I was caught up in the many activities planned for us that first weekend, and was particularly intrigued when upperclassmen performed a skit on stage during a show for us. They sang, to the tune of *Pretty Baby*, "If you're flunking out of college and you don't know what to do, have a baby, have a baby . . . ."

If Springfield, my town, was a waltz with sconces on the wall and Strauss in the background, New Haven was a rock concert with strobe lights and crashing chords pulsing from colossal, in-your-face amplifiers. At home we were basically white-bread children: most of us limited our rebellion and self-expression to light make-out sessions and a beer or two at parties. We never mixed with the bad kids, the wrong-side-of-the-tracks delinquents who, for us, simply did not exist. In this university town, however, the rules were turned upside down. Here my "social equals" *drank and did drugs and had sex . . . Oh My*! My life raft of rigid rules and solid principles was powerless to keep me afloat in this sea of swigging, snorting, screwing insanity. Expecting to meet and mix with like members of polite society, I was ill-prepared for my shocking introduction to hot hormones and men who mooned. Already the new nest was starting to fray, and my parents had yet to reckon with the mighty force of Yale.

A few weeks into the semester, they received a letter from Albertus. We are, it said, in close proximity to Yale University. Therefore, there are numerous occasions for interactions between individuals at the two schools. Since it is customary for Yale students to entertain female guests in their suites, we are requesting your consent for your daughter to visit these men in their living quarters.

WELL! My parents were outraged. Their little lily in a boy's bedroom? Absolutely not! They called me in a fury. What kind of girl would I be, to compromise myself so? And what kind of school had they entrusted me to? They were ready to pull me out on the spot. I somehow managed to calm them down enough so they'd listen and explained that we weren't exactly talking "bedroom." These suites had one or more sitting rooms as well as sleeping areas. Besides—what would I do in a bedroom that I couldn't do in the back of a car, were I so inclined? They didn't care for that line of reasoning one bit, but they had to agree with its logic. Either I will or I won't, folks! In the end, my father did not sign the permission form. Instead, he wrote a letter saying that, while he most assuredly did not approve, he would not withhold consent as he had faith in my ability to exercise sound judgment.

Scholastically I was not fairing so well, either. Having attended a few weeks of classes, I was already in trouble. For the first time in my life I was totally without direction, as no one had signed on to replace my mother. I had a schedule that told me to so I went to lectures, but as there was no one to tell me when to study, I didn't. Although the library was a very short walk from my dorm, I would not go by myself. It would be years before I would go anywhere by myself! If I needed to do research and no one else had to go to the library, the research didn't get done. Later I would be a Dean's List student, but I got off to a precarious start. Having distinguished myself neither personally nor academically, my sense of isolation grew. I stood by, paralyzed with fear, as my classmates joined clubs, signed up for committees, and learned their way around New Haven. I would venture out only if someone invited me, and she usually did only if no one else was available. I did, however, seem to get along very well with girls older than myself.

My grades improved, as did my self-confidence, which got a major kick in the butt when I met Carol Gondek, who would be my roommate for my last two years. To my great surprise, her mother worked at Yale New Haven Hospital. I had been barred from using the ice rink at Yale as admission was restricted to students, faculty, and employees. Carol and I looked enough like sisters to pass, Flo got me an ID card, and I was able to skate at The Whale after all.

Together we were a formidable duo, happily involving ourselves in all sorts of escapades. Our shared sense of humor and talent for practical jokes drove us to concoct clever schemes and act out little skits to the amusement of the other dorm residents.

Somehow, we got our hands on a walkie-talkie set. One night we hid a transceiver in the room next door. As the girls talked, we made a comment here and there. Through the wall, we could hear them, baffled, trying to find the source of the voices.

I also had a black plastic "bomb," complete with realistic-looking fuse, which when set would tick menacingly before making a loud explosive sound. We would wait until a girl was in the bathtub, and then roll it ever-so-silently under the door of the enclosure. The bang, reverberating off the tile walls, scared nine lives out of the innocent bather.

I have to give Carol credit for another bathroom prank. She had a favorite expression, from the musical *Guys and Dolls*. "It says heah in this book . . . ," spoken in a nasally drawl, usually preceded trouble. One late afternoon as we studied, she began, "It says heah in this book . . ." Turning around, I came

face-to-face with a grin more fang-like than toothy, with devilishly gleam-
ing eyes to match. "How about locking all the toilets?" "That's a rotten thing
to do," I replied. "Let's!" We slipped into the stalls, bolted each one from the
inside, and then slid out beneath the doors. Casually we went downstairs to
dinner, but the cafeteria was closed. Strange! We headed back to the floor,
only to find that a nasty outbreak of diarrhea was taking its toll on the girls
who had been unfortunate enough to eat before a problem with the food
was discovered. They couldn't use the bathroom, thanks to us. They were
not amused. We kinda were, but we quickly shimmied back into the cubicles
and opened them. No one thanked us.

Do you see what was happening here? I finally had that special friend,
that best buddy, that one girl all to myself. I blossomed. I belonged. While I
was capable of anything as long as I had Carol, I was still invisible in a group
without her.

Besides skating together at The Whale, as juniors we became very involved
in other aspects of Yale life. Members of the St. Thomas More choir, we
sang at Yale's Catholic chapel on Sundays and for special holiday concerts.
Wedged between two other structures in downtown New Haven, the small,
cozy church was red brick outside with a tall, white spire. Inside, the pale
blue brick and light wood panels created an intimate atmosphere, a peaceful backdrop for the revolution that was taking place in Catholic worship.
Though it was mandatory at the time, women didn't cover their heads here.
Common in services today but unheard of then, people held hands as they
prayed. These and other departures from accepted Church practice were
a reflection of sixties social, political, and sexual upheaval. They made the
Mass timely, relevant, and uniquely ours.

This sanctuary was also a place for me to come and be quiet—to rest,
physically and spiritually, away from the threat of student strikes and
campus protests; from the fear of academic or personal failure; from worry
about Vietnam. Here, wrapped securely in the arms of tradition, I could
cautiously flirt from a safe distance with the rebellion many of my peers

were embracing wholeheartedly. The priests bent the rules just enough to be considered progressive, but retained enough of Catholicism's age-old structure and standard rites and rituals to ground me as I watched the orderly, predictable world I always knew coming apart.

Still sweet in my memory is the snowy December night that the choir went caroling around the Yale campus. Students, and even passers-by, would join us for a few steps or a couple of blocks. After the singing, we stamped and shook the snow from our boots and coats and were ushered into a private dining room at the Yale Law School. Amidst the dark-paneled walls with ornate carved detail, leather upholstery, antique chandeliers, and huge fireplace, we might have been carolers lifted from a page of Dickens. We were served a traditional meal of lamb, which completed the feeling of other-worldliness. In an age when the North Pole was beginning to nudge the manger off center-stage at Christmas, and Santa was replacing the Christ Child as its focus, this night of sharing our song with strangers, and our meal with each other, was a simple but treasured gift.

Carol and I also performed in, or worked on, more secular Yale ventures like *Pal Joey* and *West Side Story*. We dated a few Yalies, too. Not having gone out with any New Haven area boys for my first two years of school, now thanks to Carol I could finally do what all the other girls did without a second thought.

Chapter
9

There was never any doubt in my parents' minds that I would some day marry at or above my station in life, so these boys from Yale were ideal prospects. Their futures would be secure, as mine would be should I make a match with one of them. While I enjoyed hobnobbing with the elite, as at a reception at then-Yale President Kingman Brewster's residence, I viewed it as a diversion, not a requirement.

Barely into their twenties, these young men bore the yoke of responsibility and the mantle of privilege, as well as the obligation to carry on a tradition of stupidity. Their futures were mapped out in a direct line to their fathers' law firms or medical practices. There was a definite Yale prototype. Substitute a name, a face, or even a generation, and you had basically the same individual. Though Yalies acted wild and zany, they lacked any spark of spontaneity. I saw them as dull and predictable. They did what they did because it was the thing to do, not because they particularly wanted to do it. Jaded and worldly-wise, they deemed themselves too sophisticated for innocent fun or simple pleasures. Affecting stylish boredom or contrived disdain, they got excited about nothing. Maintaining their behavior within closely prescribed parameters, most were not the authors of their lives, but merely acted out a script written for them by old-moneyed families. Lacking creative juice, they moved with too much caution to allow for unencumbered enjoyment. Lux et Veritas (Light and Truth) was the Yale motto; *Don't screw things up—maintain the status quo!* the Yalie's creed.

Completely comfortable in a tuxedo (often owned, not rented), they knew how to hold a wine glass just so, and many followed the fur-coat-and-flask tradition at football games. They debated Schopenhauer in class on Friday afternoons and got roaring drunk later that night. They dated only girls of whom Mother would approve, but a little assignation with a townie was not out of the question. (Though they could understand the most complex laws of physics or the most puzzling philosophical questions, the importance and integrity of being sexually exclusive was beyond many of them.)

In keeping with the expectations thrust upon them, most Yalies tended to limit serious dating to girls from "approved" schools: Pembroke, Vassar, Radcliffe…. Buses full would arrive at Old Eli for a weekend mixer at one or another of the twelve residential colleges. These boys had everything, from their pizzas to their women, delivered! When approaching females on campus—Yale was still all-male then—students would almost always ask first, "What school are you from?" Given the wrong answer, they would as often as not simply walk away. They seemed to feel that they owed their best behavior only to members of their own class, and they made instant and sometimes faulty judgments as to who those women might be.

Cookie-cutter counterparts of their Ivy League brothers, the Seven Sisters coeds arrived dressed in cashmere cardigans with strings of fine pearls, except for those forward-looking few who embraced the Fair Isle sweater craze of the time. Did these folks breed for the good hair gene? It amazed me that they all had the right hair—thick and bouncy, never sparse or scraggly. Even the homelier ones were attractive when their potential inheritances were factored in.

As the dancing began, so did the pre-courting ritual: the "what's-your-name-who's-your-daddy-is-he-rich-like-me" standard icebreaker. If all requirements were met, there might ensue a meaningless connection based on shared background and expectations, a pantomime of a real relationship. It's what they knew; it's the way things were done. One did not cross cultural, religious, or class lines in search of a spouse. Similar to the marriage of dynasties, families strengthened business or social ties through the unions of their children. The bond was as limp as a bad handshake—a match made not in heaven, but in the board room. Biff would no sooner wed Mary than he would marry Hortense; he wanted only Buffy or Bunny.

Most Yalies, then, did not look to Albertus girls (commonly called Aggie Maggies by the preppies) for their future mates. There was a belief and fear that Catholic school girls could not be counted upon to "put out." That prospect made even short-term liaisons with the likes of us unappealing to the horny masses.

The dates I had with Yale undergrads usually left me disappointed. Some were so full of themselves that I felt more like window dressing or an audience than an equal participant. One conferred upon himself the dubious last name of "Angst." (Carol, my roommate, still asserts that it really was his name.) I was tempted to introduce myself as Bette Sturm und Drang! Another removed his hip flask from the "Bulldog, Bulldog, Bow-Wow-Wow" context of football mania, wore it like a gunslinger would wear his trusty sidearm, and drew it just as often. He belched a lot and smelled really bad. There's class for you!

I would come to decide that these boys were not for me. I wanted the art on the walls of my someday-home to enhance the decor, not our status. I wanted us to anticipate the wonder of a life lived with and for each other, not to see the future in terms of futures and stock trading. I wanted my diamond ring to be an expression of undying love, not a sound, long-term financial investment.

Chapter
10

After two years of general Liberal Arts studies, in my junior year I began earnest preparation for my career in education. I plodded through my specialized courses with an enthusiasm bordering on catatonic. I perked up a bit when asked to select a high school in my hometown at which I would "observe" during semester break. I chose my father's alma mater, the two weeks flew by, and I began to think that maybe this career and I had something to offer each other. I was invited back to do my practice teaching the following year. Hoping to lay the groundwork for a permanent position there later, I quickly accepted. I immediately made the necessary arrangements and, by the end of the school year, my request was granted by the College. I counted down the days of summer vacation, imagining myself back in the classroom where I now felt I belonged.

Toward the end of August I received a letter from the head of the Education Department at Albertus, advising me that I would be required to do my practice teaching in or around New Haven. Compounding my disappointment, the letter stated that all the openings at area schools had been filled. Her letter closed with apologies and an offer to try to slip me in somewhere.

While I sulked, Fate conspired with the Education Department. That "somewhere" was Richard C. Lee High School in New Haven, where I knew no one. Once again I was embarking on a new adventure with no foundation, no support; but I was excited about my classes, and the school was better than I expected. Staff were so friendly and helpful that I soon felt like a member of the team. This collegial atmosphere centered around the faculty lounge, where we students were welcomed and included in every conversation.

After a few weeks I began to notice that a small group of senior boys were frequenting the lounge, behaving more like staff than pupils. They would leave the premises at will, often bringing back doughnuts or other goodies for everyone. They chatted easily and comfortably and generally made themselves at home among us. When I first saw them I instinctively stiffened up and straightened up, tilting my nose ever-so-slightly into the air. After all, I was a professional—a teacher. It took me a few days to realize that I looked like an idiot, as the real teachers were relaxed around them, treating them almost as peers. I came to my senses and began to enjoy their company, looking forward to their bantering and good-natured teasing, but there was one member of this close-knit community whom I had yet to meet.

As a college girl, I was a bit of a curiosity to these kids. The fact that I was Catholic made me even more intriguing, as they were all Jewish. I suspect that their exposure, literal or figurative, to girls outside their own religious and cultural confines was severely limited, but growing up I'd had several Jewish friends and acquaintances.

There was Ann, the only Jewish girl at our figure skating club, who took no end of delight in pointing out that she could roll out of bed fifteen minutes before we stepped onto the ice at 10 a.m. on Sundays, whereas we Catholics had to claw our way to consciousness in time for eight o'clock Mass first. Her faith and ethnic background were never an issue for the rest of us—all that mattered was whose jump was cleaner or whose spin was faster.

We also had our ice dancers—four Jewish men in their sixties and seventies who were willing partners for up-and-coming skaters. Their strong arms held us up as the deep edges they sliced into the ice with their blades forced us to carve crisp tracings of our own. These generous, patient men supported us until our competence and confidence took flight, and we were able to glide across the rink matching their long strides, sharp edges, fluid knee bends, and gracefully arched backs.

Then there was Morris, a regular at the reserved table where my dad and other attorneys met for lunch every day. I can still picture him at a Christmas party at our home, belting out carols with his Christian friends. (Though his wife, smiling politely, refrained from joining the songfest.)

So though Jewish people had been commonplace in my life for years before I came upon these students, they were just *people*. Their Jewishness was as unremarkable to me as their eye color.

But this group of boys—how fascinating they were! Cocky, and devious in a playfully innocent way, they captured the imagination of this buttoned-down, straight-laced girl. How I longed to be as free as they seemed to be. In my young mind, what set these otherwise average teenagers apart and made them so attractive wasn't their ages, or their looks or clothes or scholastic performance. We'd had cute, smartly dressed, brainy boys at my high school too. However these kids shared another characteristic—their Jewishness— and that is what commanded my attention. I was charmed by the way they peppered every conversation with Yiddish expressions, adding flavor and texture to our exchanges, and envious of the illusive something special that they seemed to share. These boys used their Jewishness in a new way. They weren't shy about it; they didn't try to mask it. That difference was a source of pride during a time when people tried very hard *not* to accentuate their differences in an effort to be accepted. Later, one of them would stand out from the others and reveal himself to me, setting a new standard for the term superlative.

Soon they were visiting me on the nearly empty campus. This was January, with most of the school on semester break. Only the few student teachers were in residence, and it was very lonely. I really appreciated the diversion! They got a kick out of hanging around a Catholic girls' college, and we became good friends. Stuart, one of the boys, often asked if I'd met Richard Isacoff yet, and the answer was always no. Curiously, if not for feisty Fate I would never have met *any* of these kids, as they all started their secondary education at James Hillhouse High School. By a quirk of residence, and the hand of Providence, they were transferred to the newly-constructed Lee High as juniors. I wondered why Stuart seemed intent on bringing us together.

I had more urgent concerns, though, and threw myself into my teacher-role. With experience came confidence and a strong bond with my students. I even began to do after-hours research for innovative, exciting material to bring to the classroom. The kids responded positively to my interest and extra effort, and my mid-session evaluation was filled with compliments.

The weeks flew by, I did not get to know Richard, and my assignment was nearly over when the civil disobedience making headlines around the country came right to our doorstep. A violent student riot ruptured the peace of my carefree, comfortable environment.

Okay, I was young and innocent, and these high school kids had dealt with student teachers before. So I refused to be taken in when they started milling around my desk that morning, saying "You'd better leave soon. There's going to be a big riot at the second lunch bell!" Happy that I was acting the professional I was supposed to be, I ignored the warnings and proceeded with the day's lesson. (Leave, indeed. How would I have explained that?) The atmosphere in the classroom grew increasingly tense as the hours passed, but this was the honors group and they stuck with their studies.

As predicted, at the sound of the second lunch bell the building exploded. Rioters ran screaming through the halls as I desperately racked my brains for a course of action. The education program had not prepared us for this. Quickly I led my class to the nearest exit and commanded them to "GO HOME." I watched as they ran from the grounds. The scene was absolute chaos as chairs were thrown through the floor-to-ceiling cafeteria windows and huge tables were overturned. More than one rampaging student crashed into me and then called back an excuse-me-I'm-sorry! (My own home-town was festering with sparks of civil unrest, which would later ignite into violent expressions of anger and hatred. I can still picture Massachusetts National Guard troops, with fixed bayonets on their rifles, lining the streets of Springfield.)

The episode earned mention in *TIME* Magazine and led the college to release us from further involvement with the school, assuring us that we'd completed all requirements for certification satisfactorily. Though our term was nearly finished, each of us decided that the real teachers would be returning to the classrooms, and so would we. With only days to go I said goodbye to my boys, unaware that my relationship with them would continue long after my time at the school was over. I discounted their promises to keep in touch, knowing how quickly the interests of teenagers can change.

Not only had I enjoyed our time together, but they had made two important contributions to my social and emotional development without my knowing it. For one thing, I was not allowed to play with boys as a child. My mother felt that there was no need, as without them in my life I'd be kept out of trouble. An only child, I of course had no brothers. I did have two male cousins roughly my age, and she felt that they provided all the inter-sex association that I needed. Since we were so close, I never considered them to be of any particular gender. They really didn't count. A few sporadic dates in high school aside, this band of little men was providing me my first in-depth interaction with members of the opposite sex!

My mother disdained roughhousing and lived in mortal fear that I might be injured, so she pushed me in the direction of "ladylike" pursuits such as coloring or dolls, preferably with just one other little girl. As a consequence of my near-isolation, in new social situations I have difficulty figuring out where I belong and have a sense of being on the outside looking in. Imagine my delight in finding myself at the absolute center of attention, and lots of it, from these boys!

But God with a plan, or Fate with a sense of humor, had one more surprise for me. Friday the 9th of February would be my final day as a practice teacher. On Wednesday the 7th I walked into the faculty lounge and immediately noticed an unfamiliar face—it was Richard. We were introduced and, though I proceeded with business as usual, not giving him a second thought, I was amazed by the fact that he was in a suit and tie. Bell bottoms were in style then, with Woodstock just a year away!

Then, the end of the week, and my time at Lee was over. As I walked past the administrative offices one last time Richard came striding out, looking for all the world like the principal himself in his formal dress. It so happened that he was basically running the school while the principal was away at a conference. Since he was a friend of my friends I said "Hi," only to be ignored. Into my mental file he went, under "a" for arrogant. I assumed I'd never see him again. (Even now he swears he didn't notice me that day.)

FALSE IMPRESSIONS

Chapter
11

eanwhile, through my participation in *West Side Story* at Yale I met John, a graduate student at the Yale Drama School. We began to date. Catholic, age appropriate, educated, and already head of his own corporation, he seemed ideal as a prospective mate. I had visited his family in Pennsylvania, and he had come to Massachusetts to meet mine. Many assumed an engagement would be forthcoming, but to me there was always something missing: the kindness and tenderness that make a relationship special. What's more, for a brilliant man he could be downright rude, crude and ignorant. When I made the trip to his home I flew into the local airport, expecting him to be there to meet me. He was not. My seat-mate on the flight, an attractive young man, was kind enough to stay with me for over a half hour until John eventually arrived. The stranger also found a skycap to take my bags. Incredibly he even had to tip the gentleman, as John neglected to do so. I was disgusted by John's annoyance at the attention I received from my companion and his failure to acknowledge the services of the skycap. There was not even a simple "thank you" to either one.

Though John did make one halfhearted attempt to seduce me, our relationship was sexually innocent. He lost no opportunity to let me know that this was not his idea of a good time. He thought nothing of saying, "I would really like a nice piece of black ass." (Had the Civil Rights Movement escaped him? Never mind that—what about basic respect for all people?) When he behaved like such an idiot, I simply ignored him. I most certainly was not in love with him, but he provided me a certain status among my classmates, reason enough to continue to date him in the absence of anyone more appealing.

True to their word, the boys continued to visit me on campus when I returned to my regular classes. The end of my stint at Lee was also the beginning of our College Weekend, and my date was another Yalie. For weeks my little buddy Stuart had been insisting, "You should go with Richard!" (WHAT? I barely *know* him, I don't even *like* him, and he's a *high school kid!*) After the very promising John turned out to be such a loser, the last thing I wanted was to start all over again with some wet-behind-the-ears little squirt. I went to the formal with my Yale escort on Friday night, suffered through the skating party on Saturday afternoon, and pleaded a headache before the folk concert that evening. My College Weekend was over, but the school's was not. Sunday was Open House, which meant that males (MEN!) were permitted above the ground floor of the dorms (remember: 1968, all-girls' Catholic college).

Thrilled to be admitted to the secret world of college coeds, Stuart and his band came to visit that Sunday and brought Richard. I found him to be a little less self-important and a bit more subdued, which suited me fine. That lasted until they offered to take a few of my dorm mates and me for a ride. We were too many and the station wagon was too small, so I kindly offered to hold Richard's camera for him as he crawled into the back of the car. Clutching the bag to his chest he adamantly declined, and my tentatively neutral opinion of him nosedived again. Later, when we were able to converse civilly, I learned that he had a Hasselblad worth several thousand dollars!

Upon our return, we all took a walk around the school grounds. Somehow Richard squeezed in beside me and managed to stay close as the rest of the group engaged in horseplay. At one point, I tossed over my shoulder the jacket I'd been carrying. Richard took it gently from me, held it open, and said softly, "Put this on—it's getting cold out." I blinked twice. Where had that come from? It was cold, but inexplicably I felt toasty-warm. I was sure my face was red, whether from blushing or glowing I couldn't tell.

Once back on campus full time I concentrated on my courses, one of which was a Drama Seminar. We were required to produce and direct a one-act play, and I selected A.A. Milne's *The Ugly Duckling*. A major problem presented itself: I needed strong males to assist with set construction and talented males for the cast. The lead was no problem— John was the obvious choice. By now our dating relationship was nearly over, but his generous offer to enhance my assignment with his theatrical expertise stood. He helped with set design and lighting, but was above the sawing and hammering that my props demanded. I turned to my kids, and they did not disappoint me. One had a supporting role, and the rest pitched in to create the fairytale setting.

During breaks in rehearsal John usually stood aloof from the rest of us, and as we worked he was often pompous and condescending to me as well as the kids. He was not well liked by them, and they especially resented his behavior toward me. Over time, little seeds of revenge began to sprout in their minds.

The group came to our tiny campus theater every night, and soon Richard was showing up as well. While the others joked and played as they worked Richard stood quietly by, asking only what he could do next. "Paint that bench" I would say, and then turn away to laugh with the others. Soon the bench would be finished and there he'd be again, looking for another project. I began to notice.

Every so often I would need to purchase materials and, having no transportation of my own at school, relied on one or the other of the boys to drive me to various stores and malls. One particular night, Richard was the one with the car and agreed to go shopping with me. Expecting no more than a chauffeur, I was amazed when he set to work right alongside me. Taking an active interest in my purchases, he sought out the best fabric;

analyzed color and patterns; and, with his photography-trained eye, came up with combinations I never would have considered. He was good! I was surprised and delighted. At some point during the evening it hit me that I was completely unaware of any age gap between us. When he suggested coffee at The Farm Shop on the way back, I accepted. Wait a minute . . . coffee? Most boys his age would suggest a Coke!

Not like a fumbling preteen graduate of etiquette class but a confident, poised adult, he stepped aside to let me pass, held doors open for me, and showed me the utmost respect and consideration. We settled into a booth and, sitting opposite him, I looked directly into his eyes for the very first time. The person I saw, looking back at me, was no high school kid. His thoughts were insightful; his speech articulate. He gave me his total attention, told me about his life and family as if he truly wanted me to know, and responded to my comments in a way that told me he was really listening. If anything I was behaving like a schoolgirl, trying to follow our conversation while taking a mental inventory. He had the most beautiful eyes I'd ever seen on a man: green with soft golden flecks. They were obliquely set, which gave him an exotic expression, and fringed with thick, lustrous lashes. His hair was medium-brown, slightly longish, not curly or stick straight. (I don't like either.) He had the exaggerated sideburns worn mostly by Jewish kids at that time—he says he copied the style of The Monkees' Mike Nesmith—which set him apart from any other guy I'd dated. With a strong nose and full lips his face was gentle, though thoroughly masculine. Was I the only one who noticed the way his smile lit up the restaurant?

I barely glanced at the waitress, barely spoke to her, whenever she came by. As efficient as a server could be, to me she was just an intrusion.

Didn't she see that I was having a moment here? This boy was damned attractive! I did not want the spell to be broken; the mood to pass.

My eyes drifted down to his hands. Did he have any idea that I was scrutinizing him so? I really, really tried to pay attention to what he was saying, but distractions were everywhere. Those hands were perfect— large enough without being paws, with a dusting of hair and immaculately groomed fingernails—a man's hands. I found myself longing to caress those hands, but how would I explain it to him? How would I justify it to myself?? I reminded myself over and over that this was just one of the boys, a high school senior, but my self was having none of it. I kept my composure and willed my mind back to our dialogue. He was sharing with me not only information, but feelings. More astoundingly, he seemed genuinely curious about things of importance to me. I sensed that he not only wanted to know about me, he wanted to know me as well. I felt a desire to wrap my arms around Richard, to protect him and keep him safe. *What was that again*? My heart felt a little tug, soft but compelling. I was more than willing to be pulled along.

I took one last, appreciative glance at his impressive shoulders. My inventory went no farther—I did not think to look below-decks. That was a blind spot for me: not that I missed it, I didn't even know it was there! (Yes, I knew that boys were different from girls, but how?) Innocence for me was not denial; it was not-knowing. Sex and sexuality were on a wavelength I simply couldn't perceive.

With no regard for the time, we were shocked to find how many hours had flown by. We hurried back to the theater where the rest of the gang waited patiently. Stuart, the self-appointed stage director of our budding romance, had a knowing grin on his face; the others, sensing something afoot, just grinned. Richard was no longer an outsider, but very much a part of our odd little group.

Chapter
12

Stuart (synonymous with shenanigans) was the ringleader and chief instigator. Naturally, I'd met him first. Small and wiry, nicknamed "The Puppet," he was constantly on the lookout for an angle, a scheme, a gimmick. Usually his exploits were more mischief than mayhem. He rigged the grille of his car with flashing red lights and also installed a radio-telephone and police siren. It always got him where he wanted to go, when he wanted to get there. At seventeen, he was a key-carrying member of the Playboy Club. You want to know how a kid managed to get himself such a prize? So do I! I never asked how these things came to be, as I was afraid to find out. Stuart enjoyed tossing Yiddish phrases about. They may or may not have been authentic—how could I tell? I do recall that his fondness for medical terms got the better of him when he mistook narcolepsy for myasthenia gravis.

Stuart appointed himself my protector, and he took good care of me. During winter break at school he vacationed in Florida, phoned me several times, and brought me a huge chocolate alligator as a souvenir. I got another memento of Florida as well, thanks to Stuart. A week or so after he returned home I received a call from the long distance operator: someone had been dialing my number, from Florida, on a stolen telephone card.

Richard and Stuart became friends in junior high school. While Richard was smarter, more self-assured, and better able to converse with adults on their level, Stuart was more outgoing and adventurous. In ninth grade, Stuart purchased an old letterpress which he set up in his basement, and the two started a small printing business with considerable success. After a while Stuart, restless and looking for a new challenge, took up with three other classmates; they comprised the group I met at the high school that day.

Neal was one of the regulars—a scratch golfer quiet, reserved, and polite, at least in my company. He was a follower as was Ira, the most ethnic-looking of the bunch. Lowest in the hierarchy was another Richard, nicknamed "Smoot." He functioned as Stuart's gofer and yes-man. It was Smoot who would find himself on stage (in tights, yet!) for my play. Neal, Ira, and Smoot were always very much in Stuart's shadow.

Richard remained friends with Stuart but was actually on the periphery of the gang, who began to engage in more daring pursuits of which he wanted no part. It was common for Stuart to drive the others to New York on a Friday night, where the drinking age at the time was eighteen to Connecticut's twenty-one. Having had perhaps only one drink himself, he had the privilege of ferrying the others back home, sick and stinking, at the end of an evening's revelry.

It was clear that Richard was not your average student, in ability or school-related activities. The only one of the five in advanced classes, he crossed the line between student and pseudo-administrator with ease. When I was in the classroom, I did not know that his was the voice I heard over the PA system each morning, reading the day's announcements. Nor was I aware that he was routinely sent by the vice-principal to make the school's bank deposits. The resourcefulness and finely honed intellect that faculty appreciated only served to distance him even more from his fellow students.

Having received little direction, encouragement, or support from his parents as a child, Richard sought affirmation from other adults in his life. By demonstrating his considerable talents to school faculty and administrators he won the validation he so craved, but failed to realize, especially from his father.

Richard was daring in his own way and, though he didn't look for trouble, he did not back down from it either. As co-editor of the school newspaper, member of the yearbook staff, and school photographer, he had occasion to frequent several rooms in the building where related equipment was stored. For this reason, he had a master key to the school. For reasons not quite so obvious, the other boys did too.

Richard was in the habit of leaving his camera in one of those rooms while he was in class. One day, going to fetch it after school, he discovered that it was missing. Though he did not know, a tuba was also gone from the band room. Obviously the boys became suspects because they had easy access to the equipment. Why Richard would steal his own camera, and what he would do with a tuba, were questions not addressed. The boys were summoned to a meeting with school authorities and the New Haven police.

All of the boys were there with their parents except Richard, who went alone. Typically, his father and mother chose not to attend. The principal sat at the head of the table; Richard took a seat at the other end. The interrogation centered not on Richard's loss of a pricey camera, but on the possession of master keys by students. Far from being intimidated, he assumed control of the discussion. He knew the system so well that, when the inquiry began, he was ready. "Were you aware," he asked the principal, "that we had the keys?" The man admitted that he knew. "Did you, at any time, tell us to give them back?" Richard continued. No, he did not. Aside from the fact that they had keys, there was no evidence that any of them had stolen anything. Seeing the facts of their case turned against them, school officials simply asked that the keys be returned. The group were suspended for a week, but Richard never handed over his keys. He did, however, bring the meeting to a close by leaning over the table, riveting his accusers with his eyes, and asking, "Are there any questions?" There were none. Richard was escorted home in an unmarked patrol car.

Richard knew what he wanted, and he knew how to get it. The massive student uprising that disrupted my practice teaching presented a major challenge to him. Seeing the events of that day unfold, he grabbed his camera bag and followed the action to the cafeteria, where he began snapping away. He had gotten quite a few fine shots when he was approached by a uniformed police officer and a plainclothes detective. "What are you doing?" they asked. He fired off a smart answer along the lines of "I'm just sitting down to lunch." Riot or no, this was the cafeteria! Again they said: "WHAT are you doing?" There he was, with two cameras around his neck. They probably could have figured it out all by themselves. He helped them: "I'm taking pictures." "STOP!" they demanded. He refused. When they persisted, Richard reminded them that they were violating his first amendment rights. They steered him firmly in the direction of the office, where they made him hand over his film. He complied, and they released him.

Don't even think you've heard the end of this story! On their way out of the cafeteria Richard slid the Nikon into his camera bag, where he expertly removed the film. He slipped a blank roll into his hand and pulled it from the bag, dramatically stretching it out so that it was exposed to the light. "If I can't have the pictures," he cried, "no one can!" If he had simply given them the blank roll, they would have known it was the wrong one. This way, they had no way of knowing that there was never anything on the film they now so smugly held. As for the other camera, the Hasselblad, it comes with a removable back which contains the film. Richard switched backs, replacing the one containing live film with the spare he kept ready, loaded with blank film. Again the dramatic "exposure" and the police left, satisfied.

Richard had his pictures, which he developed that night in his darkroom at home and sent to *The New Haven Register* the next day. He also published a special edition of the school newspaper. There followed a flurry of phone calls which never amounted to anything. Richard's exposé of an incident preferably kept under wraps caused a great deal of embarrassment to the mayor, for whom the school had been named. Richard's police department-issued press pass was confiscated.

Unwilling to be caught off guard again with another melee, school officials had police patrols in the building for the next several months. Richard and the boys would often take them out for breakfast.

Chapter
13

These kids I had become friendly with were obviously precocious, so it was no surprise to me when Stuart called one day to invite me to lunch at The Playboy Club in New York City. Tame by today's standards it was considered, at the time, the ultimate in sexual depravity among folks just out of the *Leave it to Beaver* fifties. Totally sexually naïve, I seized the chance to see firsthand this provocative place people whispered about but never admitted patronizing. If it was really that bad, I reasoned, some morals squad would have closed it down. Besides, I could always leave. I accepted the invitation and rode with the boys into Manhattan one morning. I had no classes that day, but I'm sure they did. We went anyway.

I had a moment of anxiety when we approached the entrance, fearful that the seventeen-year-old boys would be carded, or that Stuart's key would prove to be a fake. At twenty-one, I was not personally at risk to be turned away. We were ushered in without incident, and I steeled myself for the shock of a lifetime. What I saw, instead, were tables full of mostly middle-aged men having lunch. The most decadent thing about the establishment were the Bunnies. They were almost laughable. These women were dressed in pastel satin, strapless, bathing-suit type outfits cut high at the leg. Their breasts threatened to spill over any minute, but I guessed right away that those costumes probably held more stuffing in just the right places, pushing things up and forward, than the big fluffy cotton bunny tails did. The bow tie 'round the neck, shirt cuffs, and tall ears-on-a headband completed the ludicrous image.

Of course these waitresses were taught to bend at the waist to maximize the view, but they were so alike that to me it was seen-one-seen-'em-all. They were neither seductive nor alluring, just dressed up like toys to play with. Maybe the men saw things differently. All the boys, except Richard, were in awe of these creatures. He concentrated on his meal. If there were back rooms in the place with other things going on, I didn't know. We had a first-rate lunch and went home. Except for my simply having been there, the Playboy adventure was a bust. As always, though, we had great fun just being together. Again, Richard stood apart from the rest as they drooled over the impossible prospect of a side dish of rabbit not on the menu. He showed no interest whatsoever in the women. Not because there was anything wrong with him, because there was everything right with him. I liked that he lacked the superficial, juvenile curiosity typical of those men who embrace and cultivate the playboy image.

Along with our out-of-state excursions, one feature of my relationship with these boys was their delight in showing me the sights of a city in which I'd lived for nearly four years, but knew almost nothing about since few of us had cars on campus. They had mentioned a certain attraction, The Ice Cream Parlor in Westport, which was a must on their list of places for me to visit. Plans were made for us to go on a certain Friday night, but when the time came only Richard and Neal were available. Richard drove and I sat in the middle, with Neal on my right. Neal and I talked all the way, and as I glanced at Richard for some response (he was being very quiet) I noticed what a good-looking profile he had. And oh, the smell of him! Not the ubiquitous Canoe, the scent of the sixties, but British Sterling Bitter Lemon—a unique, exotic, sophisticated fragrance. He seemed to have a certain presence. Even the way he handled the car was impressive, with those strong, capable hands on the wheel. He was neither timid new-teen driver nor know-it-all jock. There was something about him: something that made me feel safe; that he was in control and I could trust him with my life. I flirted with the idea of trusting him with my heart. Not since that night at The Farm Shop had I thought of him that way, but suddenly I found myself very aware of everything he said and did.

The Ice Cream Parlor was situated in an old white house. We parked in the lot to the rear of the building and headed up a flight of stairs. To our left, as we climbed, we could see a dark room barely illuminated with lights of various colors. Kids danced to the throbbing beat of rock music that escaped into the night air around us. The atmosphere was pure '60s all the way, which left me totally unprepared for the scene at the top of the steps. We passed through a door into a turn-of-the-century fantasy land! An old-fashioned soda fountain took center stage, beyond which stood clusters of quaint little tables and chairs of wood and twisted metal design. The seat backs were heart-shaped. I remember a floor of black and white squares. Everything about the setting was true-to-theme, and I felt totally out of place in my short skirt and trendy shoes. Not usually one to wax nostalgic about history, I was completely taken in by this magical place. But magic of a different sort was happening here as well. Although I was with Neal, I began to sense that I was *with* Richard.

Neal and I carried most of the conversation, but while my mouth was working and my mind was working, they were going in two very diverse directions. I made small talk with an ease which belied my inner turmoil: *Richard's really attractive! He just seems to fill this room! What, are you nuts? Okay, he's a boy, but still . . . You're almost old enough to be his mother! Now that's a total exaggeration. Yeah, but hey—I feel a little tingly!* Richard had a magnetism that drew me to him despite logic or reason, and I found myself willing to be pulled closer. His impact on me was astounding, and my response amazed me even more. But wait a minute! One crucial part of this equation was missing. Richard probably thought of me as some older lady teacher, and there were plenty of really cute girls his age at his school.

I knew; I'd seen them. Why should I think he would be interested in me? I began to watch him more closely. I compared his behaviors to Neal's. Were his eyes holding mine just a little longer? Did he seem a wee tad more attentive? I was certain he felt something too, and I was thrilled. *Yes! There it is, just below the surface . . . a tension between us that wasn't there earlier.* No gentle flutter of butterfly wings in my stomach—I felt the frenetic flapping of a hundred hummingbirds! My heart swelled. Still, my reaction was only an emotional one. I was not yet even aware that sexual organs could generate physiological sensations, and mine weren't dropping any hints.

The Ice Cream Parlor exceeded its reputation, with its delicacies as delicious as the decor. Without fuss, Richard picked up the check. On the way back, the boys discussed the sequence in which Neal and I would be dropped off, and it was decided that Neal would go home first. When we pulled into his driveway, Neal asked me to step out of the car for a moment. Once I had closed the door, he whispered, "Richard likes you. He's going to make a move tonight. I just wanted to warn you." Richard would tell me later that he had no idea why Neal suspected, as he had never expressed an interest in me to anyone. I thanked Neal, got back in, and rode the rest of the way to campus plastered to the passenger door, waiting nervously for Richard to do something for which he'd get his face slapped. It was one thing for me to indulge my imagination a little; quiet and private, it was within my control. For him, a *boy*, to overstep his bounds was another matter altogether. To my surprise, and to his credit, he did nothing.

He walked me to my dorm entrance, softly touched his index finger to my forehead, nose, and lips, and said goodnight. That was it. No fumbling, no grabbing, no teenage pawing or sloppy kisses; just one tender, sweet, loving gesture, and he was gone.

Chapter
14

Allow me to paint the backdrop against which our little drama was unfolding. We grew up in the fifties, when life was grand. The behavioral code was strict and the moral code, loud. "Different strokes for different folks" would come later. We had a one-stroke-fits-all mentality. Everyone knew his role in society. Mirrored in the early cowboy TV shows, where the good guys wore white hats and the bad guys wore black, there were two types of people: law-abiding citizens and criminals. A decent person's most daring breach of the rules might be rolling through a stop sign or exceeding the speed limit by a mile or two per hour. Villains were locked away, and the rest of us walked the streets freely and without fear.

Marriage was forever, and the occasional divorce sparked a scandal. Men worried about bringing home only the bacon, not some loathsome sexually transmitted disease. Frowned upon, extramarital affairs were swept under, and kept under, the rug. Everyone was supposed to pretend there was nothing going on, even in the face of overwhelming evidence. One kept up appearances. No wonder the times were fraught with tension! At least widespread exchange of sexual partners was rare. Women stayed at home unless economic necessity forced them to seek employment. For most, the opportunity to stray was almost nonexistent.

Everyone had the same basic goals: move to the suburbs and buy a TV.

Every day brought with it a new convenience to make life easier, from frozen foods to automatic washing machines. Cars were enormous, with giant tail fins that would presumably, in an emergency, propel a vehicle across a swollen stream or raging river. One rung higher on the evolutionary ladder, the '58 Oldsmobile had gills as well. Post-World War II society was flourishing. There was no dissent, no protest, and really nothing to complain about.

While most Americans marched to the beat of the same drum, we Catholics stepped lively to another rhythm as well: the all-pervasive, ever-present, non-negotiable dictates of the Church. They included obedience to civil authority, of course, but reared up mightily in defense of our immortal souls, particularly with regard to sex.

Sex within marriage (there was no sex outside of marriage) was primarily for purposes of procreation. People with physical impediments to the making of babies were not permitted to marry. One's introduction to carnal pleasure took place on the wedding night. For singles, "impure touching" was forbidden, as were lustful thoughts and "occasions of sin." At least that was the ideal.

While Catholics took matters to an extreme, society as a whole was repressed as well. On family TV sitcoms, with few exceptions (Lucy and Desi come to mind), married couples were typically portrayed simply as fathers and mothers. They did not interact as husband and wife. In unisex pajamas, they occupied twin beds several feet apart, giving no indication of a sexual component to their relationship. Because television invaded the sanctity of the home, eagle-eyed censors pounced on anything that would have a negative influence on young, impressionable viewers.

When Elvis "the Pelvis" made his debut on *The Ed Sullivan Show*, his gyrating torso caused a sensation. Later, when the Rolling Stones appeared on the same stage, they were obliged to alter their controversial lyrics "Let's spend the night together." For that performance, they sang "Let's spend some time together." Though rock 'n' roll changed popular music forever, the musicians had yet to change their appearance. They still performed in suits and ties, with short, neat haircuts.

Movies were another story. Closeted away in the confines of a theater to which children typically had no easy access, they were becoming more and more sexually explicit. But we Catholics had a weapon against porn: the Legion of Decency. This organization would review films and rate them for us. Going to an X-rated show would guarantee you a spot on the devil's roster for all eternity. The R designation put you on the standby list.

I had a problem with this. How were these reviewers able to rate the movies? They went and saw them, that's how! Did they close their eyes to the nudity? Did they block their ears to the sounds of lovemaking? Or did they—just did they—enjoy every steamy scene? They had an excuse and a defense for watching what we were forbidden to see. I used to wonder where the souls of these critics lined up on the road to eternal damnation, and if they even gave a damn. Were they recruited from the Lechers' Union? To my knowledge, no Legion member ever had to be bound, gagged, and dragged into the theater.

But the double standard was everywhere. While a husband could be forgiven for a lapse of faithfulness, a wife did not cheat. Boys, being boys, might sow wild oats, but girls were expected to be virgins at the altar. There were, however, two types of girls: good girls, who *didn't*, and bad girls, who *did*. The good girls didn't really know what the bad girls who *did*, did. The choreography of sex was a big mystery. My friends and I were clueless, and the others weren't letting us in on the secret.

Never having seen any, I had no idea as to the structure of male genitals. I could not envision intercourse. I knew where babies came from—the mother's stomach—but the port of entry mystified me, and the way out was no less confusing. It's not that I was given negative information at home. My parents never said that sex was bad, or wrong, or dirty. I just wasn't told anything at all. Only once did I ask my mother about it, and she simply said, "When the time comes you'll know what to do." What I had to do for the time being was keep the boys away. Holding hands, an arm around the shoulder, a chaste kiss were all okay, but that was as far as my education would progress.

We were the good girls and had no way to get our hands, literally or figuratively, on the details of the whole sex phenomenon. The bad girls found out for themselves, in spite of impressive efforts to keep them pure. In the seventh grade at my Catholic school we had our first dance, and we were advised not to wear patent leather shoes. A boy might see reflected there something he shouldn't! In high school, when kids were more daring and danced slow dances close together, with bodies touching, the priest would walk around, tapping couples on the shoulders and reminding us to "leave room for the Holy Ghost." Even in college, until a year or two before my senior prom, a faculty committee would assess each girl in her formal dress before the big night to weed out any immodest gown in advance. I hiked up my hemlines each day like everyone else, but skirted around the whole sexual revolution thing.

So here we were, before the swinging sixties, before the disco seventies, before feminists arose and lesbians arrived. My friends and I felt the muffled rumble of marital discord around us, but our own family units were solidly intact. For us "happily ever after" was not just the stuff of fairy tales, it was the expectation of every young bride-to-be. Romance was *romantic*! A relationship had depth and character, and involved more than random copulation. It was about a feeling of connection to another person, and a desire to strengthen and enhance that bond over a lifetime of being together. Love came before sex, and sex did not happen without love. That's the way it was among my contemporaries, and that's the way it would be for me.

Chapter
15

As my dates with John came to an end, I got to know Richard better and could not avoid comparing the two. I found Richard to be a thoughtful and sensitive person with great integrity. John was brash, self-centered, and almost amoral in his behavior at times. One day I realized that, despite his academic achievements and business success (his own theatrical lighting company back home), I could not respect John. In contrast, I held in high regard this high school boy who, to the rest of the world, was so ordinary. I saw Richard's virtues all the better for John's weaknesses.

After our trip to Westport Richard began phoning me at the dorm, and I found myself looking forward to his calls. Eventually, he worked up the courage to invite me to lunch. I accepted. Waiting in my room for him to arrive that day, I heard an explosion of squeals from the lounge area. Investigating the commotion, I saw several girls hanging out the second-story windows. It seems that Richard had borrowed his father's Jaguar XKE for the occasion and was quite the center of attention! He did not look like a senior in high school, and no one took him for anything less than an area college student. We went to lunch at AL'S where, for the first time, he took my hand in his. It felt just as good as I'd imagined it would: warm, strong but soft, a bit possessive. I floated on air. My only other recollection is hearing the song *The Mighty Quinn* playing on the car radio as he drove me back to campus for my two o'clock psychology class. The professor was Fr. Quinn. Loved that XKE!

A few days later, when Richard told me that he would be spending February school vacation in Concord with his friend Ira, I was surprised at how disappointed I was. As the week started, I found myself counting the days until he returned. Play practice just wasn't the same without him, and neither was I. To my amazement he called that Wednesday, saying that he missed me and would be coming home early, on Friday. About ten-thirty Friday night he arrived back in New Haven, and I slipped out the rear door of my dorm to meet him. I arranged for a friend to let me back in later. We had coffee and joked about my misunderstanding: I thought he'd gone to New Hampshire to ski, when in fact he was at *The* Concord, a Jewish resort in the Catskills! My heart flip-flopped when he said that he'd had a miserable time because he wasn't with me.

From the start of my college career, and maybe even earlier, if I met an attractive young man I'd automatically think, "Boyfriend material? Husband potential?" With Richard, I did no such thing. Not once in the beginning did I consider him eligible in any way. Our friendship evolved naturally at first, with no expectations beyond it. As we came to know each other, not in a dating context but simply as individuals, love sneaked up on us when we weren't looking.

One night, during play rehearsal, I came down with wicked menstrual cramps and lay wrapped around myself in a fetal position on the couch. Richard disappeared. Suddenly he *was* seventeen, just a boy, unable to deal with womanly issues. To my amazement he returned a few minutes later with a blanket, which he folded gently around me. He had gone to my dorm and called the floor for one of the girls to send down something warm and comfy! The cozy glow I felt had more to do with him than the blanket.

We continued to see each other, but had to be very circumspect. I was involved with a student from the school where I'd done my practice teaching. This could be grounds for dismissal from the education program, if not the college! There would be no explaining my way out of it. So we drove around a lot, with Richard pointing out various places of interest in and beyond New Haven. We ventured out in public from time to time and managed to avoid detection. Our favorite haunts were The Spot, a tiny, off-the-street Wooster Square pizza place with a national reputation; and Jimmies of Savin Rock, then a beach-side seafood drive-up that served the best hot dogs in the world. Of course we returned to The Ice Cream Parlor too.

Although I was familiar with a few of the popular songs of the day, I had grown up listening primarily to classical music. My years at the piano and my quest for accompaniment for my skating programs kept me tuned to that station almost exclusively. When a certain song was announced on the radio one day my dorm mates erupted in hysteria, but I was clueless. It was 1964, and I had never heard of The Beatles.

It was Richard who introduced me to whole albums of Simon and Garfunkel (my favorites), The Association, The Byrds, The Beach Boys (his favorites), and others. We listened to them over and over again on his eight-tracks as we cruised the highways and byways of southern Connecticut. *Love Is Blue*, by Paul Mauriat, became our song. The "blue" represented all of the impediments to our relationship.

Because his father owned Yale Auto Parts in New Haven, Richard often came to see me in whatever car happened to have dealer plates on it at the moment. One day he showed up in a Peugeot, which promptly blew its radiator hose. Reluctantly dialing his dad's number for help, he wondered how he would explain his presence at a Catholic girls' college. His father came, fixed the hose, and never asked a question.

By my parents' reckoning I was long overdue for a weekend visit, having severely curtailed them since I started dating Richard. I usually went by train, but this time he drove me. From his car radio-telephone, we called my mother to tell her I was on my way. I put Richard on the line to say "hi," identifying him only as one of the kids she'd already heard about.

When we arrived, I invited him inside for introductions—a literal foot in the door. To my mother's credit, she knew at once that there was something more here than I was admitting. As fast as was socially permissible, she thanked him for delivering me safely and showed him out. Then she turned on me. "What is that boy doing driving you home? He's not your boyfriend, is he? (She could read me like a book.) What about John? Don't get involved with this kid and oh, by the way, we'll bring you back to school on Sunday!" But John was no more.

With final preparations for the show underway, one evening I went upstairs to the attic of the Students' Building, where scenery and costumes were stored. I was looking for a particular prop, and Richard came along to help. Suddenly I sensed him very close to me. I turned around, and he took me gently into his arms and kissed me. It was as soft and sweet as a dusting of powdered sugar on my lips. In an instant, he'd let me go. We stood looking at each other for a few seconds. Then, with prop in hand, I started down the stairs. A couple of steps behind, he paused and said, ever so quietly, "I love you." I stopped, smiled up at him, and whispered, "I love you, too." We rejoined the cast and crew with our precious secret tucked up tenderly in our hearts.

Back at the dorm, I floated through the lobby and up to my room. *Richard loved me*! Suddenly I understood with absolute certainly the expression "when he's the right one, you'll know." I *knew*! The impossibility of the situation hit me at once, but my heart was so filled with joy that I was determined to be with him regardless. The details would take care of themselves.

Chapter
16

What did I see in this boy, who was already so much a man? Yes, he was physically attractive, but that was not all. His most prized attribute was his integrity, which earned him my enduring admiration. He had intense focus, a strong sense of purpose, and amazing depth to his character and thought. Intellectual without being nerdy, he was more at home in the company of adults than with his fellow teens. He was kind, generous, and fun, with a lively sense of humor. Though so much younger than I, he naturally assumed a leadership role in our relationship, and I was happy to follow. This came about in part because I was unfamiliar with most of the area beyond the campus gate. Richard would decide where we'd go and what we'd do on any given night. I went willingly along, pleased just to be with him.

But there was more. Still scared of my own shadow, I was impressed by his confidence and the way he maneuvered out in the world. Just as my father would, he took care of me. I felt safe and secure in his company. He talked at length about cars and photography, and I learned to speak "spark plug" and "shutter speed." I even got to hold the Hasselblad at last! He drove me past the neighborhood of his youth, his early schools, the places where he played and the building where he prayed. He opened himself completely to me, sharing his history and baring his soul.

Richard demonstrated his personal integrity on several occasions. One time, when acquaintances offered to include him in a money-making deal involving the sale of stolen cigarettes, he declined and eased himself away from these "friends." In another instance he was set up by his sister Ellen and her pals, who wanted to see if he would succumb to sexual temptation. Knowing that he had not yet indulged, they sent one girl to the house on a day when he was home alone. She did her best to seduce him—to no avail. In telling me this story years later Ellen assured me that, when we married, Richard was "pure as the driven snow"—her exact words.

As much to avoid my parents as to give me moral support, Richard was backstage with me on opening night in early March. The production was a huge success (I earned an A) and, after my parents had gone, Richard presented me with an enormous bouquet. "I know how much you love orchids," he said sweetly. I thanked him profusely and fought in vain to contain the giggle that escaped my lips. What I had in my arms was a lovely arrangement of gladioli. My brain rooted around for a tactful response. I blurted out, "Uh, Richard— these aren't orchids!" It was the best I could do on such short notice. He studied the floor with all the intensity of a doctoral candidate defending his dissertation. Then, from under lowered lids, hopeful eyes searched my face for signs of a practical joke. He waited patiently, letting the drama build. With wry smile and raised brows, I gazed back at him. Finally, a tentative "Are you sure?" I was sure. But those humble blooms were as beautiful to me as the rarest hothouse flower.

John had another engagement immediately after my play performance that night. He was to direct a high school revue in a neighboring town, and time was tight. As soon as the curtain came down, he raced out of the building without even saying goodbye and jumped into his red Thunderbird convertible. A few seconds later he charged back inside, coughing and choking. The boys had arranged a parting shot for John and a show of support for me. In return for his shoddy treatment of me during rehearsals his car was filled with tear gas, courtesy of Stuart! Not pepper spray, mind you, but the real thing.

While I scolded my defender soundly for his actions, inwardly I was cheering. John had it coming. The car cleared out and he sped off, with no harm done except to his considerable pride. I never saw John again.

Once rehearsals and performances were over for all the seminar students, the theater building stood empty in the evenings. Richard and I spent hours there, talking and listening to music. I particularly remember an Igor Kipnis album of harpsichord pieces, *The Harmonious Blacksmith*. There, without the distractions of movies or sporting events, we shared our thoughts, ideas, and dreams and dared to imagine a future together.

One night, as we rode around the streets of New Haven, Richard talked about our children and what we would name them. "Wait a minute," I interrupted, "you haven't even proposed to me yet!" It was half-joke, half-hint. Conveniently, we were stopped at a red light. As he held my eyes with his, he asked me to be his wife.

So there it was: the moment when all our fantasies of endless tomorrows slammed smack up against the harsh realities of our current situation. I was twenty-one, Catholic, about to graduate from college. I was in love with a seventeen year old Jewish high school senior. We would face objections from all sides. In that moment, I even wondered—was he just a kid playing grown-up with a puppy-love first crush? Mercifully the light turned green, and we picked up speed. Richard was staring straight ahead as I gave him my answer. "That was impulsive," I said, "spur of the moment. You never would have asked me to marry you just then if I hadn't set you up like that. Take some time to think about this and then, if it's what you really want, ask me again." He agreed.

Chapter
17

Before we met, when Richard envisioned a future for himself, what he saw was a lifetime of work. He could not imagine a personal life, did not anticipate amorous relationships, and certainly did not entertain thoughts of marriage! The example of his parents' union made that option less than appealing. He'd be too busy. He would live alone, in an apartment, with a television (of course!); many, many books; a desk for working at home; and a darkroom. He never even considered a pet. I have asked him, "Do you think you would have been happy like that?" He answered, "At the time I would have said, 'I don't know what "happy" means.'" Sad, depressed, and scared, he avoided his emotions. To feel anything was to feel pain.

"I had no expectation of romance at all," he will tell you now. But by listening, paying attention to, and caring about what he said, through my interest and encouragement, I gradually earned his trust. Until then, he was standoffish. He could not consider romance, let alone emotions, until there was trust. (I, of course, was totally unaware of what was going through his mind.) But then, suddenly and without warning, trust was there, with romance firmly in its sights.

I saw him the next night and the night after, and the subject of marriage did not come up. But I was doing a lot of thinking myself. Was it God's hand at work? Something had moved me to change career plans; to make a haphazard college selection. Something had placed me, last minute, at the high school he went to by chance, where we were destined to meet. What made me return to the classroom after being excused from further teaching due to the riots? Why did Stuart persist in bringing Richard to my campus, night after night? Against all odds, we had been drawn together. I had no notion of us as star-crossed lovers, nor did I see our relationship as the kind of romantic tragedy from which tearjerker movies are made.

Did I love him? With all my heart. He challenged my mind and soothed my soul. I was already a better person for having known him. I would not cave in to societal expectations but would marry this dear, gentle man. Our love would be an example to be emulated rather than ridiculed.

Exactly one week later, during a drive in the country under a starry sky, Richard pulled the car to a stop alongside a snowy field. Resting his hands lightly on my shoulders, he drew me to him in a gentle embrace. With great tenderness he asked, "Will you marry me?" I could see that he had given the matter the same careful consideration as I, and also arrived at the same inevitable conclusion. We belonged to each other.

I was not through with him yet. "How do you know?" I persisted. "How can you be sure, at seventeen?" His reply stunned me. "I asked myself, if you were to become incapacitated to the point where I would need to care for you, would it be a burden or a joy?" As he opened his heart to me, I could see into the depths of his soul. "It would be a joy," he said. Unhesitatingly this time, I said yes.

We sat for a while, awed by the momentous promise we had just made. I gazed out the window at the field, which suddenly sparkled as if set ablaze by brilliant moonbeams. Had some celestial bride tossed her diamond-dotted, sequin-strewn wedding dress into the night sky, only to have it float to earth and settle *right there*? We kissed and hugged, crying tears of joy and giving a prayer of thanks for the great blessing we had been given, the gift of our love.

He placed nothing on my finger, as his part-time earnings at his father's business would not cover the purchase of an engagement ring. And he couldn't very well ask his parents for a loan! Ring or no, I was ecstatically happy. It was March 26th, exactly seven weeks from the day we met.

Chapter
18

Alone, we carried on like any other betrothed couple. To everyone else we were still simply acquaintances. One person who was onto us early in the game was Mabel McAvoy, my housemother. With appearance and demeanor suggestive of a Yale bulldog or two in her lineage, she was really a sweetie, with a large heart and generous spirit. Over the years she had seen many of her girls dropped off after dates, past curfew and drunk, by area college men. She liked and trusted Richard, knowing I was safe with him. She appreciated the fact that I always came back sober and on time.

Until one night, when we went to a drive-in to see a double feature. We had his mother's car, and kept it running much of the time. The late evening spring air was nippy and we needed the heater. When the movies ended, Richard could not start the car. "We're out of gas," he said. "Uh huh," I replied. *Oh, sure,* I thought to myself. I played along, waiting for a little action. Curiously, he seemed more preoccupied with the dashboard than with me. Still, I couldn't resist. With eyebrows raised, I teased, "Not very original! Is that the best you can do?" No, he insisted, the tank was really empty. Unaccustomed to the Chrysler, he had trusted the gas gauge, which still hovered at the quarter-of-a-tank mark.

He made a few calls. We got a little help and pulled up to the dorm just before 2:00 a.m. (My curfew was midnight.) Puzzled to see so much activity at that hour, I remembered in a flash that it was College Weekend at Yale. Albertus girls attending functions at Old Eli did not have to return until two. Striding into the lobby and past her office, I beamed a brilliant smile at Mabel. With a sincere good-night, I headed for the elevator. I half expected her to call me back because she knew I had not been at Yale, but she kept my secret.

One evening Richard and I approached the dorm after a night out and came upon a few girls lingering outside, afraid to stagger past the house-mother in their inebriated condition. One of them was a foreign student from Haiti named Viviane. Sidling up to Richard, she slurred, "Ummm—I like your pants!" (He had a body that would do any pair of pants proud.) Knowing him as I did, I was surprised that he did not seem the least bit embarrassed by this overtly sexual comment. The next day I asked him why. He thought that she was simply, literally complimenting an article of his clothing! She wasn't. Then he was mortified, and didn't want to face her again. Viviane was equally horrified when I reminded her of the conversation, having remembered nothing once her hangover was over. She didn't want to see him again either. Eventually they were able to laugh about the incident, but never to each other.

Easter vacation was torture for us, as I was home for five days. As soon as my parents left me back at the dorm on Sunday, the 22nd of April, Richard picked me up. We would usually see movies in out-of-the-way towns, or find new little restaurants where we were not liable to be recognized. It mattered not what we were doing, as our greatest enjoyment was in being together. But this night we sat in the car on campus, and he seemed to be in no hurry to go anywhere. He took a velvet box from his pocket and opened it to reveal a small, round diamond in a Tiffany setting. He was as proud to slip that ring onto my finger as I was to have it, but I couldn't wear it in public. Back in my room later, I shared the news with my roommate and another close friend and trusted that it would remain safe with them.

Even among people who liked each of us as individuals, there was amazement and disbelief that we were actually pursuing a serious relationship. Unfailingly respectful and polite to us, they gossiped behind our backs and had great fun at our expense. (Okay, the concept was a bit difficult to grasp, I admit.) In time, though, we-as-a-unit were accepted fully. Reservations melted away.

Prom talk began to dominate dorm conversations: who was going, and with whom? I had a decision to make. For many of my classmates image was everything, and most of them did not know Richard well, if at all. A Yale date was highly prized, as were boys from the military academies or other Ivy League schools. At the very least, the guy had to go to college somewhere. Could I bring Richard as my escort for the dance? Would I be ashamed of him? If this was a test, I passed with flying colors. So did he.

On prom night he held his own against the intellectual giants of Yale— discussing political theory, government affairs, and current events with the best of them. We had a lovely time and made quite an attractive couple in our formal attire. We had an idea: why not take this opportunity to visit Richard's parents, as they and I still had not met? Richard called to let them know we were coming as I fixed my makeup and hair. He truly believed that they would embrace the girl he loved so much. But there was no answer at their home, so the introductions would have to wait for another day.

The other day came soon enough. We were running out of time before I'd be graduating and leaving New Haven for good. We selected a particular night, and Richard told his mother he'd invited a teacher from his school for a visit. Although in 1968 the uniform for twenty-something girls was miniskirts and go-go boots (and I had my share of those), my wardrobe featured a more classic style. I looked the part of an education professional when we arrived at his house. His mother and father, Doris and Paul, were waiting to meet me before leaving for an engagement elsewhere. She was gracious and welcoming. He studied my legs.

Then his mother reminded Richard of his manners, saying, "Take the lady's coat." *The lady?* It was clear that she viewed me as Richard's elder. Not a peer, and certainly not a fiancée! I knew we were in trouble.

Once they were gone, Richard showed me the home he shared with his parents and two sisters—a sprawling, eight-room ranch adjacent to the country club. Off the foyer to the left were three bedrooms. If you are a whiz at math, you have probably deduced that mom and dad occupied one bedroom, the girls claimed another, and Richard had the third. An admirable conclusion, but wrong. To the right of the foyer was the general living area. Past the kitchen, at the far end of the house, was a back hall, laundry, and garage entry. Beyond all this, by itself, was Richard's bedroom. While the girls' areas were apparently planned by a person purporting to be a decorator, Richard's space was plain and uninviting. His obvious physical isolation from the rest of the family struck me at once, but I would not learn until much later how very strong that symbolism actually was. His mother would explain the separation as an attempt to give Richard some "privacy," as he'd soon be going away to college. But really, was he a family member or a boarder?

Richard's seven-year-old sister, Mindy, spent the evening with us. As the hours passed, she and Richard grew tired. We were sitting on a long couch in the family room, Mindy to my left and Richard to my right. After a time Richard lay his head on my leg, stretched out on the couch, and fell asleep. He must have looked pretty comfortable, for soon after Mindy was mirroring his position on the other side. Happy that they were so relaxed and not wanting to disturb them, I simply sat quietly, pleased to be spending time in Richard's home with part of his family. I heard the door open when his parents returned, but could not move away quickly enough. Okay, part of me didn't want to! His mother walked into the room first. She took in the scene, and what was unspoken, spoke volumes. I don't know what she was thinking, but it couldn't have been good. I did not go back to the house again that year.

Bette the college girl,
near graduation.
Albertus Magnus College,
New Haven, CT, 1968

Richard the high school boy, senior year.
Richard C. Lee High School, New Haven, CT 1968

Bette, sometime around 1949.

Richard, sometime around 1953.

Bette, age 17, in 1963
Member of Little Sun Valley Figure
Skating Club, West Springfield, MA.

Carol, my college roomie at
Albertus Magnus College, 1967.

Stuart "The Puppet" Rosenkrantz,
our matchmaker. Senior photo from
Richard C. Lee High School, 1968.

*The Honorable
Tullio A. Francesconi . . .
Upon retirement from
the Bench, Trial Court
of the Commonwealth,
Springfield, MA age 75.*

. . . and his alter-ego

*Dad and Bette at Little Sun Valley Figure
Skating Club's Halloween party, 1963.*

Arriving in the area between City Hall and the Auditorium before his speech, Dwight D. Eisenhower is surrounded by Troy T. Murray, left, Tullio Francesconi, Mrs. Eisenhower, and Sen. Henry Cabot Lodge, Jr.

Veronica, my mom, age 75, 1985.

Harry, the patriarch of Richard's family, with his second wife, Fanny around 1967.

Richard's parents, Doris and Paul, around 1968.

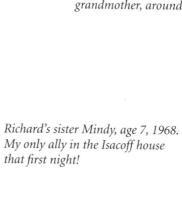

Lena, Richard's eccentric grandmother, around 1991.

Richard's sister Mindy, age 7, 1968. My only ally in the Isacoff house that first night!

Our wedding at St. Anthony of Padua Church, Wilmington, DE. May 2, 1970.

Wedding Kiss at the magnificent bronze doors of St. Anthony of Padua Church.

*Showing dogs became
a family affair.*

Kira at Annapolis (MD) Kennel Club show, 1988, age 8

*Richard at Chesapeake (MD)
Siberian Husky Club, 1985*

*Bette at Holyoke (MA)
Kennel Club, 1989.*

Chapter
19

Let me set out here the cast of characters I would eventually come to know. Embroiled in a relationship more complicated than you could ever guess, Richard's family might have been the role model for a classic Greek tragedy.

Doris was one of two children born to a man who fled Poland to escape the pogroms. The son of a rabbi, he lost many of his relatives in the Cossack raids, and later others to the Nazis. At seventeen, Harry Tashman journeyed to America and made his way doing menial labor. Eventually he took a wife, Rose, found for him according to custom by a New York marriage broker. This same matchmaker would pair him with his second wife, Fanny, after Rose passed away.

Harry relocated his bride from New York City to New Haven, where with a partner he founded what would become the multi-million dollar grossing Elm City Plumbing Supply. Possessed of a strong work ethic, he devoted himself to the pursuit of enlarging his business and increasing his earnings. Harry did not spend his money. It was a family joke in later years that he brought all his considerable fortune to the bank, after which as far as he was concerned the bank owned it.

Short of stature, with an annoying habit of smacking his lips as he spoke, Harry cast a long shadow over the rest of the family. You've heard that money talks? His bankroll bellowed—and everyone fell into line. Cantankerous and self-absorbed, he had to be center stage at all times, refusing to share the limelight. I recall a family holiday dinner many years later, with all assembled fussing over our two-year-old daughter, the first grandchild. After a while, we noticed that Harry had disappeared. He was found in another room, by himself, sulking and pouting because his only great-grandchild had stolen the scene. Of course he had to be cajoled, flattered, and enticed to return to the festivities. No one dared scold him for being jealous of a little girl. You can bet he was not ignored again that night.

On yet another occasion, when we were up from Maryland for a weekend, Doris asked that we bring our daughter to visit Harry at his business on a Saturday morning. "He is so anxious to see her!" she said. And so we set out on a cold, damp February day, with sleet pelting the pavement. In her little dress and coat Kira was shivering from the chill, and we hurried her inside. We were escorted through the showroom and into a cavernous, barely heated warehouse-type office, empty except for a desk at the far end. There sat Harry, reminding me at once of God on His throne. We came forward with deference when he acknowledged us, and he reached for my baby to give her a gooey, wet kiss. That was it: the end. No more.

Harry turned his back on her, directed his attention to Richard, and began to talk about the business. He did not address me or my child again. For the better part of two hours I tried to amuse her, knowing all the while that she was as cold and bored as I was. After about two minutes we had taken inventory of the entire area and went out to the showroom. How fascinating can sinks and tubs be? We pretend-flushed each toilet about a dozen times, until that got old. Finally I approached the two men—he was not *my* grandfather—and told Richard it was time for her nap. He got the hint, and we left. Now wouldn't it have made more sense, since Harry had quickly gotten his fill of his great-grandchild, for Richard to have brought us back to his parents' house and then returned to continue the conversation? There he was, a grown man, a husband and father, riveted to his chair and afraid to move until dismissed. Such was the power of Harry.

Obsequious to his face, people often were downright devious behind his back. Perhaps it was simply convenience, or maybe it was their way of retaliating. I recall the hot dog incident: at a family barbecue, I was made to promise that I would represent the wieners as kosher, even though they were not. Harry's concerns were often dismissed as petty when it could be done covertly.

Yet as large as he tried to make himself appear—much as an blowfish does in the face of a predator—I saw Harry as a frail elder. Even a home movie, shot when he was just fifty years old, shows him dressed in ill-fitting suit and fedora, toddling unsteadily around the backyard after the family's puppy. He neither impressed nor intimidated me, but I always treated him with kindness out of respect for Richard's feelings. Richard deeply loved the old man, who showed him more affection and attention, albeit limited, than anyone else in the family. Richard had already fulfilled his grandfather's dream of a male grandchild. But there were more expectations: another rabbi in the family, perhaps, or a fine doctor? And, of course, marriage to a nice Jewish girl. Months after our wedding, when I finally met him, Harry said, "Richard is like Jesus Christ to me."

About Rose I know almost nothing, as she died before I came on the scene. Richard remembers her as a wonderful grandmother, though he is unable to provide specifics. Doris told me once that she was not fond of her mother. She did not elaborate.

To his great disappointment, Harry sired no sons. He had scant interaction with his own little daughters. Coming home after a long day at work, he would slump into an armchair with the newspaper, barely noticing the eager youngsters clamoring for his attention. In the Eastern European style, he was the provider. His wife ran the home and raised the children. Despite his riches, the girls owned only two dresses apiece. They could not have been unaware of their father's preference for a male child. Their mother, in awe of her husband, hovered in the background of their lives. The emotional deep-freeze that I would feel so many years later was not lost on the sisters.

The elder daughter, Doris, was wed first at age eighteen. She married Paul Isacoff, a twenty-two year old Navy veteran of World War II. It was inevitable that they would meet, as their families knew each other. The lad's father, Louis, left Russia with his four brothers and two sisters, also settling in New Haven. He established Yale Auto Parts, another financially sound company. By the time Paul was seventeen, when he escaped his home to enter the service, his mother had divorced and remarried. Lena was big, boisterous, and bossy, with wild carrot-colored hair and rhinestone-studded glasses. At about a thousand decibels, her voice was in perpetual overdrive. Independent at a time when women weren't, she went to work at her second husband's drapery and fabric store. After she left him, she hustled dresses for a small salary plus commission. There would be yet a third husband; a third divorce. Lena, too, had suffered abuse when young and would come to practice the child-rearing techniques that were so familiar to her. She, like Harry, would exact a toll for her affections.

This came home to me with striking clarity early in our marriage. One Saturday morning, as I lounged in bed, the phone rang. It was Lena, whom I had never met or even spoken to. She was at a friend's house in Springfield, having come from Pennsylvania for a visit. But she would be staying with us for the week, thank you. As an enticement, she added that she had brought a wealth of gifts, including many items from the drapery and fabric store. Never mind that she had no idea of our decorating tastes or color schemes.

Panic plopped itself squarely into the middle of my peaceful day: Richard was at his monthly National Guard training weekend, and I didn't know Lena. What would I do with her for seven whole days?

"Let me call you right back," I said and quickly contacted Richard, claiming a family emergency. (It was!) He reached his grandmother and explained that, as we both worked, we would be unable to entertain her for the week. We would be delighted to see her that evening and the next, though, when Richard was through with his Guard duties. He would get back to her later to make arrangements. When he tried, she was gone. She had retreated to

New Haven to lick her wounds. We followed immediately and groveled and fawned as she held court, doling out forgiveness in tiny increments. Harry and Lena were the stars around which the family orbited, at once drawn to and repelled by his quiet insistence and her brash demands. She could not understand why her offer of many gifts did not buy her entrée into our home and lives.

A Navy medical corpsman assigned to a Marine unit, at nineteen Paul Isacoff served in the Pacific Theater, Guam, and Iwo Jima. He was sent to Nagasaki after the bombs fell. As if the resulting horror wasn't painful enough, the teenager had to stand by helplessly while people were incinerated with flame throwers. The devastation he witnessed had a marked and lasting impact on him. Until late-onset Alzheimer's tapped his long-term memory of the facts and mercifully capped his reservoir of associated feelings, he refused to discuss his experiences there, though he did return to Guam in 1995 for a fiftieth anniversary reunion. Back home after living the loose life of a seaman, he marched straight into a society with rigid moral expectations and little tolerance for emotional display.

The only emotion Paul could express was anger bordering on rage. Though in 1950s America the war was over, it still ravaged his soul. Stuffing down his feelings, curtailing his wanderlust, he proposed to the young Doris. As sex was not as freely available then, nor as readily condoned, many men returning from war married for easy and legitimate access. Whether Paul was one of them I cannot say, but if he was in fact enthusiastic about marriage, I suspect that he was totally unprepared for fatherhood.

Doris beat her younger sister to the labor room. Thirteen months after the wedding she delivered Richard, her first baby. If her new husband was less than pleased to be tied down so soon with parental obligations, her father was ecstatic at the arrival of the long-awaited male heir. At a relatively young age Paul had to redefine himself, from young buck/playboy/stud to husband and father. How staid! How old and dull and weighty! He faced the sobering truth of his new responsibilities with a longing backward glance at youth, freedom, and carefree self-centeredness. At the same time, though, he valued work and learning as much as play. He joined his father at Yale Auto Parts, of which he would eventually assume ownership. After undergraduate study at Quinnipiac College, he took a master's degree in business from Trinity College in Hartford. Working long hours, he never took time off except for business-related pursuits. On Sundays, when the place was closed, he drove around looking at cars. With few friends outside of family and coworkers, he was more comfortable among inanimate objects than people.

As ambivalent as Paul might have been about increasing his family so soon, imagine Harry's overwhelming joy when his daughter presented him with his first grandchild, a boy! Richard's launch into life was not a gentle one—he was propelled into existence by a boot in the ass. In essence, he was given away. As least that's the way I see it, and I have my reasons, though I can't prove it. Doris literally, if not physically, presented Richard to Harry.

Finally, the brilliant light of her father's approval shone brightly upon her. At last, she outdid her mother in pleasing the man for whose affection they both competed relentlessly. I firmly believe that the symbolic gift of Richard was Doris' way to atone to her father for having been born a girl, and to her husband for tying him down so soon in their marriage. Years later Doris would tell me, "I always thought I wanted a boy, but then I had my girl . . . ." This child, Ellen, would be hers alone, not to be shared with her father. All the love, attention, and devotion possible was lavished on that middle child, that *girl*, who arrived three years after her brother. Richard was figuratively set aside in the Isacoff household. He was Harry's boy. Mindy, nine years younger, fared little better.

Ignored by her father, as she simply didn't exist for him, Doris learned to hide away thoughts and feelings which were never acknowledged or validated. As she would say, "I stuffed them in a closet and slammed the door behind them." She accepted, nourished, and cherished her role as victim. Nearly paralyzed by the tight grip she kept on her emotions, she showed neither anger nor love. A certain swagger in gait, accompanied by a tic at the corner of her mouth, were the only clues to her displeasure. Librium was her best friend and constant companion.

Paul, too, had learned not to be direct in expressing what was on his mind. He channeled his frustrations from early abuse into great explosions of anger. Constantly on the lookout for attack, he adopted an "I'll get you before you get me" attitude and was ever on the offensive. The preemptive strike was his best weapon against emotional pain. He always came across as aggressive and antagonistic. He even liked to categorize himself as "an equal opportunity hater." Never would he give a compliment when an insult would do. I once made chocolate chip cookies for Richard when we were dating, and Paul told me that they were not very good. (Famous Amos could have hand-delivered a special batch and would have gotten the same response.) Looking him straight in the eye, I replied, "You needn't have had any. They weren't for you." That was the beginning of a tit-for-tat relationship that actually served us rather well for a long time.

My husband was not strong enough to handle him, and my young daughter was totally defenseless. One memorable time, when she was quite small, Paul came home to find Kira in Doris' arms. In dark glasses and hat, with beard and pipe, he was a scary figure. When he boomed out a huge hello, my little one burst into tears. Rather than quiet down he hollered, in disgust, "Ah, what's the matter, you big baby?" There was no concern, no gentleness in his manner whatsoever. She screamed all the louder. He ramped up his volume, too. "Oh, for Pete's sake!" he snorted. Still trying to be the good daughter-in-law, I looked to Richard to do something. I saw the ambivalence in his eyes: concern for his distressed child could not override his fear of standing up to his father. He said nothing.

Later, when our daughter was about five or six, Paul would twirl her around in a revolving chair until she begged him, crying with fright, to stop. Again disregarding her feelings, he laughed at Kira and told her that his kids enjoyed it when they were young. And again Richard stood quietly by, but this time I did speak up—and took to watching very carefully her subsequent interactions with him.

Although Doris seldom failed to elicit the mandatory kissy-kiss that heralded our arrivals and departures, they seemed more like empty gestures than tokens of genuine affection. The contrast in behavior between my parents and Richard's was never more striking than in their welcomes upon our visits from Maryland, where we lived for eight years. Usually pulling in to New Haven around 11:30 pm, having left home after work on a Friday night, we would find an all-but-dark house, the occupants asleep. Letting ourselves in with the hidden key, we might come upon Doris emerging from the bedroom to greet us. Paul was nowhere to be seen, saving his hellos for morning. After a perfunctory "How was your trip?" she would open her arms to our daughter and say, in a flat, monotone voice, "Oh, precious, come to grandma." A few moments on the lap, and Kira was packed off to bed. Reasonable late at night, but the routine did not vary if we came at noon on a Saturday. This only grandchild might spend a few minutes with her grandmother in play, or examining knickknacks and other attractions in the house. In short order she would be plunked down in front of the TV, to idle in neutral while Richard and his parents discussed the family business . . . echoes of our time at Elm City Plumbing.

Contrast all of this with our trips to Springfield, and keep in mind that my father and mother were old enough to be Richard's parents' parents! Often getting there at one o'clock in the morning, we would find lights blazing throughout the house. As we slowed to a stop, the door would burst open and my dad and mom, then in their seventies, would come flying out, tripping each other in their attempts to get to their beloved grandchild first. They would nearly tear her apart, each wanting to be the first to hold her, and hug and kiss her. From the minute we arrived, I had no daughter. My parents took over, and life in the house revolved around her for the entire time we were there. She was in gear, and she was engaged. My dad took her fishing, to the circus, and to a *Sesame Street Live* show. They fed the ducks together and planted a little tree. They had their special breakfasts at McDonald's. One summer, during an Olympic year, my parents built an entire track and field course in their backyard and held Olympic games for her! These were complete with a winner's podium and awards. Mom took my dad's old high school medals—some actually in track and field—and hung them on red-white-and blue grosgrain ribbon, just like the real thing. The love shining through all of these endeavors was palpable.

No doubt Doris and Paul did their best with the cards they were dealt. But their capacity for warm, loving relationships with their only son and granddaughter was severely limited by their own unresolved issues. Today's standards would categorize them as emotionally abusive.

Chapter
20

Too soon, for it would be the end of life together as Richard and I had known it, I was taking final exams in anticipation of finishing my college education. We were beginning to worry about what we would do once I was back in Springfield. We had no doubt that things would work out, but the details were becoming unmanageable.

I had not secured a teaching position for myself because I hadn't looked for one. But one came looking for me. Every few weeks that spring, representatives from various Connecticut high schools would visit our campus to recruit prospective graduates. I generally ignored the notices of upcoming sessions as I lived out-of-state. Windsor High School caught my attention, however: it was just south of the state border which touched Springfield on the other side—an easy twenty minute commute from home! I met with their delegation, and it seemed to go well. I would hear from them again.

We had one fun night left, and that was Richard's high school prom. Although we arrived together, he walked in with his friends. I found teachers I had known during my stint at Lee and stood with their group. Like them I was dressed in street clothes, so I looked more like a chaperone than someone's date. As it was no secret that the boys and I were friends, I meandered over to them after a decent interval and risked one dance with Richard, since a few of the other faculty were dancing with students. There was a girl named Nancy, sitting with her parents, who could not take her eyes off Richard. I knew about the crush she'd had on him throughout senior year. I encouraged him to ask her to dance, knowing she'd remember it for many years. The glow in her eyes told me I was right.

Graduation week was upon us, with constant parties and rehearsals. I tried to see Richard as often as I could, especially since the time we had left was so limited. On my last Sunday at school Richard came to pick me up, bearing six dozen daisies. Every night that week he brought more flowers, until by Wednesday I had thirteen dozen bouquets! I had to move them out of my room to the lounge, which by then smelled like a funeral home.

The day of my graduation was bittersweet. Though I had come to love my school and to appreciate everything these last four years had given me, the pride and satisfaction I felt at finishing college was tainted by my parents' animosity toward Richard and their anger at me. With all my heart I hoped that they would put aside their negativity for the occasion, so that we all might share in the joy of my celebration together.

With some amusement I recalled the circumstances that brought me to this school, and my chosen field of study, four years ago. I recognized that there was a purpose to it all. I firmly believe that Dad had some Divine guidance when he insisted that I go into teaching, as that was my first gentle shove in the direction of Richard. Could they get their minds around the concept that things happen for a reason? That this was meant to be? It wasn't going to happen this day, that's for sure.

A Commencement Mass in the morning preceded the awarding of degrees that afternoon. The religious service was held at St. Mary's, a magnificent, ornate edifice in downtown New Haven affiliated with the college. Richard went alone and sat by himself in an otherwise empty pew. It was the first time he had ever been inside a church. Certain that he was the only Jewish person there he huddled, feeling small and terrified, looking for a place to hide.

With a grand prelude resounding from the enormous pipe organ, an honor guard bearing the school standard and other banners started to process solemnly to the altar, followed by the rest of the student body. As was the custom for all formal school functions everyone, freshman through senior, wore black academic regalia. When the last girl had been seated, the Mass began.

As Richard would tell it later, his perception was very different: *thunderous chords, not unlike those in a Vincent Price horror movie, heralded the onslaught of an army of black-robed figures, the vanguard of which brandished spears. They were coming for me, and I was trapped!* He was sure it was the Inquisition all over again.

He survived the morning, only to face a greater challenge after lunch. This time the threat was real, with the enemy determined to prevail. Richard came to the campus and found my parents and me on the lawn, visiting with classmates and their families to exchange greetings and congratulations. Seeing him, my mother took me aside and hissed, "I don't want him sitting with us for the ceremony!" I snarled back, "Well, he's going to." And he did, though not a word was spoken among the three the entire time. My attitude was, hey—you are going to be related soon, and you'll be together for the rest of your lives, so you'd better learn to get along.

Though my fantasy celebration included dinner for the four of us at an elegant restaurant, my parents suddenly felt an urgent need to get an early start back to Springfield so as not to be traveling after dark. (Since when?) We loaded the car, with unwelcome help from Richard. His flowers filled the entire back seat and, it must be said, they stank. Many were almost a week old by then, but I didn't care. He gave me a wonderful camera as a graduation gift, all the more special because of his strong interest in and talent for photography. We said our stilted goodbyes (a kiss would have been really awkward with the wardens hovering about), and the car drove off.

I barely noticed the ominous silence as we rode along, so consumed by misery that all I could do was cry. I mourned the end of an idyllic spring with Richard, not knowing when I would see him again. Spotting a promising restaurant in Hartford, my dad pulled off the highway. It was dinnertime, and my parents wisely understood that some acknowledgment of my achievement was required. In public a certain modicum of civility would be maintained, enabling us to mark the milestone event without the accusations and recriminations that were sure to follow later. We spent a somber hour with them picking at their food and me snuffling into one tissue after another, my meal untouched.

Back home I retreated to my bedroom, with stuffed animals from Richard gathered in my arms. After a time my mother came upstairs to say that he had called, but she thought I was sleeping and told him so. I did not get to speak to him.

She then handed me a check for forty dollars, saying that I could buy myself a London Fog raincoat as a commencement gift from her and my father. So this was to be my punishment for loving Richard! There is no question that, had it not been for our relationship, I would have been given a new car for graduation and a splendid party. As it was, I spent the night alone. I did not cry myself to sleep, as there would be no sleep for me. I just cried.

From my mind's dusty file of useless facts I learned at college leapt a Psych 101 term: approach-approach conflict. I dearly loved my parents, and their expectations weighed heavy upon me. I did not want to hurt or disappoint them, and I knew I was doing both. I ached for the carefree relationship we had and wanted us to be close once again. I was torn in two; my loyalties were divided.

I was one hundred percent my parents' daughter At the same time, though, I had promised myself to Richard wholly and entirely. Though I had experienced many crushes and a few puppy infatuations, he was my first love and would be my only love. I knew this without a doubt.

His courtship of me had ruined it for any prospective future suitors. I could not bear the thought of losing him *or* Mom and Dad. What was I going to do? Desperation, fear, and panic careened around wildly in my head, crashing into each other and producing explosions of terror. I curled myself into a tight ball and lay, with chattering teeth and shivering limbs, watching the sun rise.

With the new day came a new resolve: whatever it took, I would work things out. Though I had never openly defied my parents before, I would forge bravely ahead and trust that their love for me would keep them close. They had given me life, but my life now was with Richard.

Since my parents had made it clear that his overtures would not be welcome, Richard and I arranged for me to call him over the summer. It would be our only means of communication. During vacation I returned to a part-time job I'd had for several years, working in the cash office of Forbes & Wallace, Springfield's largest department store. One sympathetic coworker offered the use of her mailing address so that Richard could contact me. Any time my parents left the house together, I would hurry to the pay phone at a drugstore about a quarter of a mile from home, hoping to speak to him. In turn, he would send me cards and letters in care of my friend Joyce.

Meanwhile, Windsor High School administrators clearly recognized all I had to offer their English program and invited me to visit their facility. After a cursory second interview the job was mine, with much handshaking and congratulations from them and dumbstruck thank-yous from me. I would start in September, teaching the entire ninth grade and one class of juniors.

At home, I spent all my waking hours listening to Richard's record albums, which he had left with me. More than any other, the music of Simon and Garfunkel sustained me through those dark times. Like Richard they were young Jewish men, yet they sang of church bells, rosaries, and (as I repeatedly tried to assure Richard) "Jesus loves you more than you will know . . . ." Their plaintive melodies were a soft echo of my melancholy feelings; their exquisite harmony reflected the seamless blending of our diverse lives into a relationship of stunning symmetry; and their sweet, sweet love songs spoke the words to me that Richard, because of our separation, could not. Years later, thirty-four years married, we moved heaven and earth—shook every ticket tree in the Northeast—to attend their *Old Friends Reunion Tour*. All those emotions—the love, longing, fear, uncertainty—came flooding back, but through the filter of time and distance. They were just a memory now, and we were together. After all the tears and all the years, Simon and Garfunkel and the magic—theirs and ours—are still there.

Toward the end of August Mary Anne Sullivan, my best friend from high school who was holding my hand throughout this ordeal, had an idea: why not go to Cape Cod for the weekend? She needed a break from her summer job, and I was desperate for some stress relief. Bless her, she did not object when Richard asked to join us there. We arrived first, and I trembled in anticipation of seeing him for the first time since I left New Haven in June. Would he still feel the same? I had no reason for concern. When he pulled up, he jumped out of the car to embrace me and presented me with a box. In it were letters, at least one for every day we had been apart. They were filled with declarations of love and promise. A measure of his deep devotion, this thoughtful gesture touched my heart. The weekend flew by all too quickly, and we parted company again.

We arranged a rare secret meeting for his eighteenth birthday in Windsor in early September, and I gave Richard a special present that was handmade by a craftsman from a pattern I had provided. The gift was a wooden cross about twelve inches high, mounted on a stand. Superimposed on the cross was a large Star of David. I had first seen the design on the cover of the book *Michel, Michel* by Robert Lewis. To me it represented the joining of our lives and blending of our faiths. It would also serve as a reminder to us of our commitment to each other. We were once again facing a lengthy separation, as he would soon be entering Clark University in Worcester as a freshman. Though continuing to live at home, I had started my career as an English teacher at Windsor High School in Connecticut. We did not know when we would see each other again since Richard did not have a car at his disposal, and my parents' diligence would preclude my driving to Worcester to visit him.

Fortune smiled on us, and after a few weeks Richard was able to keep a car on campus. He was still not welcome in my home, but managed to meet me a few times that autumn at a small park in Windsor when my classes were over for the day. This came about because of the Jewish High Holy Days, which are observed in the fall: first Rosh Hashanah; then, ten days later, Yom Kippur. In his travels between New Haven and Worcester to attend religious services he would detour to northeast Connecticut, where the high school is situated. Once the holidays were over and he settled back in at Clark, I did not see Richard in Windsor again.

My parents thought otherwise. Though they had no specific knowledge of our dates in the park, they rightly suspected that we were arranging to see each other secretly. I rented a box at the Windsor Post Office, where I was able to receive mail from Richard without my parents' knowledge. I checked the box every day on my way home from school and was never disappointed. As part of my job commitment I was required to lead extracurricular activities and chaperone school dances; I was also expected to attend team sports events. The drive from Windsor to Springfield took no more than a half hour, and whenever I was any later they would insist that we had been together. Ironically, this was every time *but* the four afternoons we had actually met!

Tensions increased and tempers flared as they continued to make accusations, and I persisted in my denials. One night I left to supervise a dance, and afterward went out with several other teachers to enjoy a street fair that I recall as "Windsor Days." Shops were open, and vendors had set up stalls outside as well. There was lots of food and plenty of activity. We all had a great time, and I arrived home at twelve-twenty in the morning.

My parents were waiting up for me, and began to demand that I admit having been with Richard. They were highly emotional and totally unreasonable, but the simple truth is that they were mistaken. Richard had been nowhere near me that night. Sadly, they were not interested in the facts. Only a confession would satisfy them, and it would not be forthcoming.

They were relentless and, for the next five hours, they screamed, they cried, they did their best to make me feel guilty. "What are you doing to us?" was an oft-repeated refrain, along with "You're going to kill your mother (or father, depending on which parent had the floor at the moment)!"

By daybreak, they realized that their threats and entreaties had shaken my spirit but not my resolve: I could not let go of Richard. I had given him my heart, and I would not take it back. They ordered me to break up with him, but I held my ground. Desperate, my father played his trump card.

In some earlier conversation with my mother I must have related the story of the lunch date I had with Richard, when he picked me up at my dorm in the Jaguar. Evidently she'd passed it on to my father, and he remembered it now. Hoping I might be more enamored of the car than the driver, my father made what he thought was an offer I couldn't refuse. "If it's a Jaguar you want," he said, "I'll buy you one. You don't have to go out with that kid to ride in a fancy car." Enraged, I spat back, "Keep your damned Jaguar—I don't want it." He had insulted me as well as Richard with his bribe. I would speak no more that night.

We were obviously past the point of no return on this issue. Weary and teary, we went to bed.

Chapter
21

The following days brought with them a new set of problems. In the funereal atmosphere my mother and I walked around red-eyed; my father sat stone still with teeth clenched. They predicted nothing but disaster for me with Richard, and I saw only heartbreak without him. The pressure was beginning to take its toll on me: I couldn't sleep, wouldn't eat, and had difficulty in class. Concerned about my fragile emotional state, and with nowhere else to turn, I sought counseling with a Springfield psychologist, Dr. Irving Frank. I chose him from a listing of therapists in the Yellow Pages, in part because of his Jewish-sounding name. I thought he would be more likely to approve of Richard, and perhaps be able to intercede for us with my parents.

Our first meeting consisted mostly of information-gathering on his part. When I explained the situation he seemed at least neutral, if not enthusiastic. I came away with the feeling that we would have an ally.

At my request, Richard was allowed to attend the next session. I wanted Dr. Frank to see us together so that he could recognize and appreciate that our love was genuine. We spoke for about an hour, during which time he was nothing but supportive and encouraging, albeit with typical clinical reserve. After a few more visits I was even more confident about Richard and me, but nothing had changed at home: the pressure to leave him was constant and intense.

With my back to the wall, I started getting braver and more defiant. Invited to Clark for a Saturday, I agreed to go and informed my mother of my plans. Although I drove my own car, technically it belonged to my father. Unwilling to give him a chance to deny me the use of the vehicle, I decided to go by bus. I went so far as to call a taxi for a ride to the terminal. Amazed that I had the determination to follow through, and fearful of my returning to the downtown bus station alone late at night, they offered to pick me up. I accepted, and felt that they had just thrown me the tiniest olive twig (the branch would come way later).

Richard started to drive to Springfield from Worcester every weekend. He would pick me up at the house, though I could not invite him inside. Usually we just rode around and talked, stopping for pizza or sundaes. Pushing his luck, he also began phoning me at home. We agreed on a specific time, and at the appointed hour I would be standing by with one hand on the receiver, ready to answer before my mother or father did. After a while they stopped trying to intercept the calls.

Around this time Richard began to frequent two ladies of the evening, who were most generous with their favors and would give him anything he wanted. (Sorry, I'm playing with you here.) This matronly, motherly twosome were Dot and Ann, late-night counter staff at Howard Johnson's Restaurant on the Massachusetts Turnpike in Sturbridge. Usually tired, always hungry, he would stop there for a short break on his return trips to school. Soon these angels were anticipating his arrival with fresh coffee on the burner. Although his standard order was a hot fudge brownie sundae, they would have given him a five course meal had he asked. Everything was always on the house (I don't think the house knew). After he graduated, we went back to HoJo's with thank-you gifts. At last I was introduced to these wonderful women, who had taken such good care of my fiancé. We've never forgotten their kindness.

By now it was late fall and getting colder outside. On November 30th, my birthday, Richard came to celebrate with me, bringing gifts and a cake. Realizing that cutting and serving in the car would be tricky, rejecting a park or roadside picnic table for fear of frostbite, and knowing that he was barred from my place, he rented a room at the Holiday Inn for my party. In all innocence we drank a little toast and ate a slice (or three) of cake.

Once again my parents were armed and ready when I got home. "Someone was passing by the Holiday Inn," they accused, "and saw you there." They wouldn't tell me who "someone" was, but I suspect that it was they who had been driving around looking for us. Of course they assumed the worst. Condemning Richard for compromising my honor (not to his face—they still wouldn't let him in!), they went on to remind me of my father's position and his reputation, which I had just most certainly destroyed.

I let them have it! "You would allow an animal in this house before you would open the door to Richard. We have nowhere to sit and talk now that the weather is bad. If I as an adult cannot receive guests in my home, I will have to find another place to live." How would they explain that to their friends?

At an impasse again, I suggested that they had better have a conversation with Dr. Frank themselves. They agreed and set up an appointment for the first week in January. I couldn't imagine what had transpired, but after that day all sanctions against Richard were dropped. His calls would be put through and his letters delivered; we could visit at home. Elated, I did not think to question why.

If not friendly toward Richard my parents were at least civil, and polite in the most formal way. He started making the drive from Worcester on week nights as well as weekends and managed to keep up his grades through the end of the first semester. In between, we phoned and we wrote. I canceled my Windsor post office box.

By the end of the month pleasantries were being exchanged, and I could detect a subtle but unmistakable change in my parents' attitude toward

Richard. There was the occasional tease, the rare joke. This probably had more to do with the fact that he was, and is, an eminently likeable person than with their willingness to back down. In spite of themselves, they were coming around.

Chapter
22

Then, in early February, another setback. When we returned home from a date one evening, my mother asked to speak with Richard. Gently, almost kindly, she told him that our love could not be. Her first concern was not that he was Jewish, or not Catholic, but simply that we were of different faiths. "Your side will never accept her," she reasoned, "and our side will not accept you. Will you go to separate services, both go to each, or not go at all? How will you raise children?

"Besides," she went on, "you are only starting college. If you do not finish, you will be tied to second-rate jobs forever. You will never be able to provide the lifestyle our daughter expects and deserves, and that we want for her. You are away at school now, with a lot of young (she didn't say Jewish) girls closer to your own age. You'll meet someone new to love. And you are still immature, only seventeen! You're just a boy—how can you know what love is?" (That's what I thought too, until I got to know him.) "Marriage is hard enough between two people of similar backgrounds. You will each find a partner more suitable, and will get over each other in time, if you break it off now."

We began to counter her arguments. We have a strong faith in the same God, we said, and ultimately, everyone goes to God his own way. For all of our differences there are many similarities, and we will focus on these. We are respectful of each other's beliefs and practices and have a few in common. We hadn't yet worked out the worship details, but I still attended Mass every Sunday at home, and he continued his occasional Sabbath prayers at synagogue. Regarding children—I was committed to raising them as Roman Catholics, but that discussion was ongoing.

As for Richard's career and future earning potential, it was apparent how much about him my mother did not know. His thirst for knowledge was unquenchable, and his commitment to education unshakable. If he had to switch to part-time classes, night school, or another variation of the traditional college experience, he would graduate.

There was no question that either of us might meet someone else to date, and even marry, but we could never duplicate with any other person the great joy and special relationship that we had together. Our futures apart would be ordinary at best, but too painful even to contemplate.

I saved the meatiest argument 'til last. "*Who* won't accept *whom*? Anyone who truly cares about me will care about the man I love, and whoever cannot accept Richard is not really on my side at all. Besides, Richard's family are not harassing us like this, so it's just your relatives that are a problem! We don't need them; we don't need anyone but each other."

Though unmoved she seemed genuinely sorry, even sympathetic. But she brought the conversation back to the beginning: you have to end this now, and the quicker you do, the less traumatic it will be. Do it fast, and do it soon.

Richard had an idea. "What if," he offered, "I do not see, speak to, or contact Bette in any way for a full year? That should be a good test of the depth of our love and the strength of our commitment. If at the end of the year we still want to be together, will you step aside and not stand on our way?"

Hey! He had not consulted me before presenting this option, and I panicked. Total separation for an entire year? I couldn't do it. Then I thought of that separation, multiplied by a lifetime. My mother and I answered "no" simultaneously, though for very different reasons. Disappointed, she said good-night to us. Shaken, we said good-night to each other, and he headed back to Clark.

I caught up with mom before she could slip into bed. What was going on? Just when we thought things were okay, she dropped this bombshell. I insisted on the truth, and she finally came clean with excerpts from the meeting with Dr. Frank. I had long since stopped seeing him, as my physical and emotional symptoms had disappeared once the pressure from my parents eased.

But all was not as it seemed! Condensed, this is what he had told them: "You have sheltered and protected your only child all her life, not allowing her the normal interactions with boys that other girls have. She is socially immature in this area and feels safer with a younger male than with someone her own age. This is not a serious romance, although she may believe that it is right now. The more you try to stop it, the harder she will cling to him, and you will actually force them closer together. You will have given them a common cause to fight against (did he mention *Romeo and Juliet*?). Back off and, when they no longer have anything to prove, the fire in the relationship will burn itself out." With a conspiratorial laugh he added, "They'll never marry, so please do not be concerned. She just needs to grow up, and then she will fall in love with a man."

So that's what was going on! I was outraged. I was irate. I had been betrayed by a therapist of excellent reputation whom I trusted. As it turned out, in my estimation he was neither ethical nor professional. No wonder my parents had so dramatically reversed their position after talking with him! Based on his advice and predictions, they revoked their restrictions and stood by, eagerly watching for signs that our interest in each other was waning. When it didn't happen, my mother decided to tackle the problem directly, addressing her concerns to Richard this night.

Now we were both confused: I after learning that, far from being supportive, Dr. Frank had actually tried to sabotage our marriage; she upon realizing that his prognosis for our relationship was far from accurate. If anything, it was getting stronger.

Why, when this situation was causing my parents so much consternation, were the Isacoffs taking it in stride? We had been dating for nearly a year by now, yet they showed none of the anguish and concern that my mother and father so clearly demonstrated. In startling contrast, they did little more than smile indulgently and poke fun at the disparity in our ages, but voiced no concrete objection. They may even have been relieved, as Richard had not dated extensively in high school, and his father had gone so far as to ask if he was "queer." They were probably hoping that their son would gain some experience with me, social and sexual (they didn't know me very well), eventually settling down to a lifetime partnership with a suitable Jewish girl. Supremely confident that nothing permanent would come of our relationship, they did little to discourage it.

I sensed a big change in both my parents once they understood that they had been duped by the psychologist. Now Richard's presence in the house was commonplace and, though there was little communication among the three of them, I swear I detected an occasional smile from one or another.

Chapter
23

During midwinter school vacation in February, I had surgery for removal of a benign breast tumor. Upon returning to my bed from Recovery, I saw my parents on one side of the room and Richard on the other. No one was speaking, but all three rushed to my side as I was wheeled in. Richard showed me a lovely bouquet of red roses he had brought, and the nurse scurried out to find a vase. Clumsily he began to stuff the delicate blossoms into the container until my mother, a talented designer, could stand it no more. She offered, he accepted, and she arranged the flowers in a beautiful display. I was grateful for the small interaction.

That Saturday my parents were to attend a dinner-dance and did not want to leave their recovering daughter at home alone. Richard would stay with me, I informed them, and they reluctantly agreed. I had wanted to cook dinner for him but, with one arm strapped to my side by a tight binder that circled my chest, I was seriously handicapped. To my great surprise, my mother prepared a wonderful meal in advance and left everything to warm on low heat. Her reasoning dawned on me later: if we were eating, we wouldn't be doing anything else! She was ever the worrier and guardian of my chastity, even though I was in a good deal of pain and rather encumbered. Richard set the table, served us, and cleaned up afterward. He had great fun playing house.

We continued to date throughout February and decided to surprise my mother with a party on her birthday. That night, the parental antennae went up when we secreted ourselves in the first floor bathroom for over an hour. "Come out!" they demanded. "Wait!" we replied. They were ready to pounce when we finally emerged. (Unlike Richard's parents, who would condone and even encourage sexual activity, mine expected a virgin bride on their daughter's wedding day.) Their apprehension vanished when they realized what we had been doing: blowing up balloons and preparing little favors and other gifts. We had a lovely celebration, helped along by the Harvey's Bristol Cream we gave Mom. Life was good.

Then the snows came, and once again my mother found cause for vigilance. One late winter night, as Richard backed out of our driveway for the trek back to Worcester, his rear wheel burrowed into a gargantuan snow bank. No amount of coaxing, shoveling, or swearing would free it. After an exhaustive effort, he admitted defeat and came back inside to call a towing company. There was a mighty blizzard raging, and the trucks were already out in force, with lengthy waiting lists. The answering service would not even take a name, so sure were they that their men would not be able to do any more jobs than those to which they were already committed. The last place he tried, with the unlikely name of Green Hornet Towing, would make no promises, but noted the address and said they'd do their best to fit us in. We settled down to watch for the flashing yellow lights.

By now it was after midnight, and my parents were ready for bed. As was their custom each night, they turned the thermostat back to around sixty-two degrees before retiring. They said good-night (to both of us? I couldn't tell) and went upstairs to bed. Within minutes, of course, my dad was snoring. But my mother could not rest! She knew we were sitting together on the living room couch by ourselves. Never mind that we were bundled up in ski pants and heavy parkas, ready to dash outside when the Greet Hornet showed up. Never mind that sixty-two degrees on a summer day is a whole different animal from sixty-two degrees in a dark house late at night, when the outdoor temperature is ten. We were shivering, we were freezing, and the only huddling together we did was strictly for warmth. But she wasn't taking any chances. Eventually she fell asleep and I guess we did, too. The Green Hornet didn't come.

In the morning the car was still stuck, and it was becoming apparent that it would remain so as radio bulletins were advising stranded motorists not to rely on tow trucks. There were just not enough of them to go around. My dad went into the garage to putter for a few minutes, then called Richard outside. Together they managed to free the obstinate tire. But that was nothing compared to what was going on inside the house: my mother was cooking an elaborate breakfast, and it wasn't for my father or me! She wanted to give Richard a hearty meal before he left for school. That was it; that was the turning point. He was now officially at least my boyfriend, if not yet my fiancé.

During this time I usually wore the diamond ring Richard had given me only when I was not at home, and if it was not liable to be seen by anyone who could cause us a problem. Sometimes I had it on but would turn the stone to the inside of my finger so that it was obscured by my hand. One night in March, my mother came up to my bedroom for a chat and asked how things were going. I told her that we would still be getting married, to which she challenged, "He hasn't even given you a diamond!" I whipped that ring out of its hiding place and flashed it before her eyes, at once proud to show it off and relieved to be through with the subterfuge. She remarked about its size (a quarter of a carat) but had no other comment. Sitting quietly, she digested the reality that Richard would be joining our family. I tried to reassure her: "Do you think you did a good job raising me?" The answer, of course, was yes. "Then have some confidence in my ability to make decisions that are right for me." She couldn't argue with that.

Although the fact of our actual engagement was never mentioned by my father, I am certain that he was informed by my mother fairly soon thereafter. By this time they had to admit (only to each other, never to me) that

Richard was indeed a special individual who truly loved me and just might turn out to be a fine husband. They were still, however, not ready to release the news to the extended family.

My mother had seven brothers, and four sisters to whom she was especially close. There was intense competition among them when it came to the accomplishments of their children. The four elder cousins (of whom I was the youngest) had all taken piano and figure skating lessons and, of course, were all college graduates. Discussion about the relative merits and achievements of each was ongoing among the siblings, and hyperbole was the norm when it came to their own. It was obvious that they were living vicariously through the next generation. Remembering back almost a year ago to Memorial Day, my mother knew that the welcome and respect accorded to John, my Yale Drama School date and guest for that weekend, would not be forthcoming for Richard. No matter how much she had might have warmed to him, it would still embarrass her to present a now eighteen-year-old to the family as her future son-in-law. She was most concerned, though, about how her elderly father would react. Born in Poland, he had many old-country values and ideas. That I was marrying a Jewish boy would mean she had somehow failed as a parent. She dreaded the look of sadness in his eyes when he learned of our plans. So, for the time being, the engagement remained a secret among the four of us.

The news leaked to the family by accident, quite literally. In the spring of 1969 I was again hospitalized briefly, and an aunt came with my mother to visit. Distracted by pain, I was unaware that I was wearing the diamond. Eagle-eyed, my aunt Mary spotted it right away and asked, "What's this?"

There was no denying what it was! Her discovery nearly did my mother in: not only was the secret out, but my aunt's husband owned a jewelry store, and this ring was from a competitor. She had only one question: when do I get to meet him? Tiny gasp . . . *so far, so good*! As for the ring, all was forgiven when I explained that Richard had made the purchase in New Haven before he knew that I had an uncle in the business. Mary wasted no time in passing the news around, and soon other aunts were clamoring to meet him.

The first to invite us to her home was Alice, also my godmother, who had always been my favorite. We went happily, thrilled that we were beginning to enjoy the status of any normal engaged couple. A woman of strong religious faith herself, Alice recognized Richard's deep spirituality and innate goodness at once. Her husband, Pete, seemed to like him as well. *Big damned sigh of relief!* Their son Jay was too young to form an opinion either way.

The rest of the family fell one by one under the spell of Richard's charm, until only my grandfather was left. While my mother still made apologies and excuses, my aunts and uncles refuted them all. Bolstered by their support she finally brought Richard, with me, to see her father. Although my grandfather spoke broken English, he and Richard understood each other perfectly from the start. I am not exaggerating when I say that it was mutual love at first sight! Years later, surrounded by eleven of his children as he lay dying, his thoughts were of Richard. He needed to know, from my mother, if Richard had gotten his bar exam results yet.

Like a reluctant bather dipping a tenuous toe in the water, my mother ever-so-slowly eased Richard into the family instead of embracing him wholeheartedly. She did not know that, while she still held back, they would soon be taking matters into their own hands. When fall turned into winter and New England weather got bad once again, Richard faced another season of treacherous commutes between Springfield and Worcester. There were nights when she'd wish him a safe trip back, not knowing that he was traveling only as far as an aunt's house, where he had been invited to sleep over!

Chapter
24

While Richard was being drawn into my mother's large family, he had yet to meet my father's relatives. There were three siblings: my dad was the middle child, with an older sister who lived in town and a younger brother residing in Arizona. With my parents, we went to visit my aunt Eden (called Edna) one night. Introductions were made, and she immediately pulled out a kitchen chair. Smiling at Richard, she pointed. "Sit!" she commanded. "Have something to eat!" Richard fell in love all over again—first with my aunt, and then with her cooking.

At the same time, I was making next-to-no progress with Richard's family. They still humored me as the current, but certainly not permanent, girlfriend. Of course as long as he was away at school they did not know the extent of our involvement, but now he had completed his first year at Clark and was home for the summer. He continued to visit me in Springfield, and I began traveling to New Haven as well.

I had left teaching for a position in the juvenile probation service. After two terms with my students, I felt that I had gotten to know them pretty well. One freshman in particular intrigued me. Not especially bright, he was enthusiastic in class, participated fully, and was always ready with an answer—usually wrong. He did his homework religiously and applied himself diligently to every project. Understanding that he had done his best, I passed him with a generous "D." Soon it was Christmas vacation, which I spent at home in Springfield. As soon as I returned to school, I recognized a profound change in this boy. Now surly, uncooperative, and disruptive, he presented a major challenge to my novice teaching skills.

When the period was over, I called him up to the desk and invited him to tell me what was wrong. He stood quietly, avoiding my eyes. He offered no excuses, no explanations. Perplexed and frustrated, I dismissed him. At the end of the day, I brought my concerns to the vice-principal. I barely spoke a sentence when he held up his hand to stop me. "You are from out-of-state, aren't you?" he asked. "Then you've been gone for two weeks and probably haven't heard. Richie has a paper route. On New Year's Eve he asked his brother to deliver the newspapers, because he would have his first date that night and wanted plenty of time to get ready. Along the route, his brother was struck by a car and killed."

I turned chalky white in disbelief and grief, but remorse quickly flooded my thoughts. While I was trying to force Richie to focus on English, he was carrying this terrible burden of loss and guilt. The romantic notion of children as empty vessels, waiting to be filled with the lofty knowledge we teachers nobly impart, was shattered. The vessels before us are not empty! Many are filled with the emotional detritus of divorce, financial crisis, childhood abuse, death, disease, or injury within the family. How could I ever take nouns and verbs seriously again in the face of such trauma? How could I dare to ram participles down the throat of a child choking on the pride he swallowed when the eviction notice arrived?

On the spot, I tendered my resignation. Because I was under contract, I remained until the end of the year. I would teach again, but never children. Determined to work directly with troubled teens and their problems, I waited for communication from the Trial Court of the Commonwealth that there was an opening for a Juvenile Probation Officer. The offer of employment eventually came, and I would enjoy that profession until the day I got up to go to work but was taken to the hospital's delivery suite instead.

In the meantime, I continued working at Forbes & Wallace, now as a computer programmer. I had money to burn and happily spent it on my wardrobe. I was particularly fond of the creations of designer Victor Joris, who was with Cuddlecoat at the time. Taking full advantage of the employee discount, I purchased each Victor Joris outfit that came along (the sales staff would put aside every one of his creations, size six, for me). I went to New Haven many times that summer, exquisitely dressed, which made a good impression but also accentuated our age differences once again.

One day, late in the season, I arrived at Richard's house without remembering (consciously or not) to take off my engagement ring. As soon as I realized my oversight, I quickly turned the stone inward. Was it too late? If his mother saw the diamond, she did not acknowledge it. To this day, I have no idea if she noticed. Like it or not, though, his parents were getting used to having me around. I think they were beginning to recognize the inevitable. I was more than a passing romance. Their son loved me, and his intentions were serious.

I have my own ideas about why the Isacoffs were so reticent to accept me as their daughter-in-law to be. They could have been afraid that I would wage a campaign to convert the entire family to my faith (though I did not). They may have assumed that I would expect Richard to have a dozen children (we only had one). They might also have thought that he would be denied a full and satisfying sex life by this repressed Catholic (no need to worry about that either).

Mindy was away at summer camp, and we were all going to participate in Family Day with her. I was surprised to learn that Richard's paternal grandmother from Pennsylvania was also in town. I wanted, well, a "grandmother"—warm, soft, and cuddly. Lena, who never quite forgave him and me for our reluctance to have her visit, was loud and (dare I say it?) obnoxious. Her presence dominated the room. Invited to sit with her, I perched on a stool at her feet, hoping for a little chat about the man we both loved. What I got, instead, was a birthday gift wish list! She wanted Chantilly for her upcoming celebration, and plenty of it. She suggested that I write down her favorites: dusting powder, cologne, etc., until she had ticked off seven items. She told me I could mail them to her. I did.

The next time I went to Connecticut, Richard met me at the door. His Alfa Romeo needed repairs, and would be going to the shop that afternoon. I said that I would stay behind with his sisters while he brought the car in. As it happened, the car would not be ready the same day, and Richard called his mother for a ride home. She invited me to come, and as we rode along I could sense her dancing around an issue of obvious importance to her. Then she popped the question: would I be converting to Judaism? Like a baying hound with his prey caught in a tree, she had me cornered.

Richard had given me a tiny, silver Star of David, which I wore on a chain around my neck. This may have prompted her to think that I was contemplating a change of religion. After briefly considering a leap from the moving vehicle, I decided to stand my ground. I hastened to assure her that this was not the case; that I had been brought up as a practicing Catholic; that my parents and I attended church every Sunday without fail; and that we lived our faith at home. "We are not religious Jews," she responded, "It's more cultural with us. But it would make everything so much easier." Convert for convenience? Never! (In striking contrast, at no time did my parents suggest, to me or to him, that Richard become Catholic.) My status in the Isacoff household suffered a serious blow that day.

It never really recovered. In my innocence, I expected our families to blend seamlessly. I looked forward to holidays spent together: an opportunity to learn about new beliefs and customs and to enhance our understanding of each others' cultures. I certainly didn't expect my in-laws to attend church, but was confident that God would not smite them for sharing Easter dinner with us. We could enjoy the more secular aspects of our celebrations, such as Christmas stockings and gifts. As it turned out, the participation was strictly one-sided. Not once, ever, did Richard's mother wish me a Merry Christmas, though his father and sisters did.

One time, I stood by and watched as she struggled to wrest a menorah from the back recesses of a kitchen pantry. "I haven't lit this thing in fifteen years," she remarked. A retort came to me, which I stifled: "Then why are you lighting it now?" Doris turned to my daughter and began to tell her the ancient story of the one-day supply of oil that miraculously lasted eight days. Kira interrupted with typical childlike impatience: "I *know* that already!" "How?" asked Doris. "Mommy told me all about it." My mother-in-law shot me a look of surprise tinged with grudging acknowledgement.

The family, myself included, gathered around the kitchen table as she said the prayers and struck the match. This scene was repeated year after year, and Chanukah presents were also distributed. As I opened mine, I couldn't help wondering: was Doris really oblivious to the fact that she was totally ignoring my holy day? Was she pretending I was Jewish too? Or did she simply not care? It would be a long time before I saw what was right in front of my face all along. I had been merely tolerated by my mother-in-law, never accepted.

Of course while we were dating, these problems were still a long way off. The difference in our religions was the elephant-in-the-living-room. My parents were horrified, his parents chose to ignore it, but we embraced it as an object of curiosity and wonder. I had to ask myself, though, if our families' objections would come back to haunt us later.

I set the romance of it all aside and expressed my concerns to Richard. How, honestly and truly, were we going to handle an interfaith marriage? He gathered my small hands between his own, and I felt like a tiny bird cradled safely in the palm of its Maker. "Do you think we met by chance?" he asked, though he needed no answer. "Or do you believe that it is God's plan for us to be together?" I knew with all my heart that this was true. Folding his comforting arms around me, he rested his chin on my head and whispered into my hair. I felt his voice, soft and soothing, caress my soul. "Then let's put our trust in Him, and let Him work His miracles."

I was astonished and humbled, all at once. Here I, the Catholic girl who attended religious schools kindergarten through college and went to Mass every Sunday, was voicing doubts while Richard, who lived a mostly secular life, had just demonstrated a faith so profound and pure.

I began to think about the religion thing some more and realized that, while I had no objection to Richard's being Jewish, I did have a problem with his lack of participation in any regular formal practice. Also, I had laughed off some of Richard's misconceptions about Catholicism early in our relationship (a favorite of ours was that Catholics pray to statues). Now I knew that, if our marriage was to work, we'd have to understand each other's beliefs. I decided that we would attend Jewish services on Friday nights and Sunday Mass at Mt. Carmel Church, where I sang and played the organ. As we would be sitting high up in the choir loft, I could talk to him throughout the Mass without disturbing anyone. It would be a perfect opportunity to explain what was going on as it happened. So we began our religious studies, and it wasn't long before I was enthralled with the beautiful music I heard at the synagogue. I would fool around with the notes on my piano during the day on Saturday, and by Sunday morning it was ready to debut at church. Many Masses were celebrated to the accompaniment of these haunting Jewish melodies, and neither priest nor congregation were any the wiser! Meanwhile, the horrible fear that had gripped Richard on the morning of my graduation was losing its hold as he became more familiar with the goings on at Mt. Carmel.

I thought it was important for us to have a common prayer to say together. The obvious choice was The Lord's Prayer, as it made no mention of Jesus. Not knowing that Richard was familiar with the words from his days at summer camp, I printed them on a balloon for him to learn. Of course, his father found the balloon and made his displeasure known.

Chapter
25

Overall we enjoyed a relatively carefree summer, thinking that we had survived the worst and believing that the remainder of our path to the altar would be, if not strewn with roses, at least not littered with thorns. That is not to say, however, that we lacked for adventure! Take, for example, the Eric incident.

My mother was known in the family and community as the cleanest woman alive. She would not permit my father to hire domestic help, as she would feel obligated to clean before the crew came. They might find a mote of dust lurking somewhere! She'd have to clean again after they left, as no one could measure up to her standards, thereby doubling her work. It is no surprise, then, that I was not permitted to have a dog—my fondest desire as a child. I begged, I pleaded, I saved up my own money, but the answer was always "no." "Someday when you're married and have a home of your own," she'd say, "you can fill it up with dogs." Though she didn't mean it, of course, I would do exactly that.

But I came close to pet ownership. In the summer of my tenth year, my mother was hit with a nasty gastrointestinal virus. Bathroom fixtures vied for her attention as waves of vomiting and diarrhea sent her scurrying to the porcelain time after time. As she grew weaker she became more frightened and asked me to call my father at the office, but I knew that he wasn't on intimate terms with the first aid manual. Between bouts, chilled and shivering, she sat on a lawn chair and baked in the afternoon sun, willing warmth into her battered body. *Noooooooooo*!! A vision of long-ago sacrificial worms in their death-nest stormed my brain, this time with Mom in the middle—a tiny, dried-apple doll remnant of the woman who used to be my mother. I would not let her go the way of the worms!

I took over her care with more authority than I had a right to assume. Recognizing that she was dehydrated, I demanded that she drink glass after glass of water. Whether or not my treatment made any difference, she slowly began to feel better and gave me full credit. In an emotional display of gratitude, and an uncharacteristic lapse of vigilance, she offered me "anything you want" in return. She suggested a train ride to New York City, or perhaps a new bike. I did not miss a beat. "A dog!" I exclaimed to her and the heavens. At once she recognized the magnitude of her miscalculation in believing that I would settle for anything less than the pet I'd always wanted.

True to her word, she sent my father and me to the pound that Saturday morning. Such was the importance of the day that I still remember it was the fourth of August. I selected a four-month-old female that I now know was a yellow lab-terrier mix. The shelter called it a collie-shepherd, as most mongrels were designated at the time. We kept her outside, but she was allowed in the garage at night. I played with her and took her for walks, but mostly I just stared at her, unable to believe my good fortune. I had my dog at last!

It did not last. I came home from my first day at school in early September to find that my dog was gone. Mt mother stood by, strangely quiet, as I searched frantically for her. Finally, she spoke. "Daddy took her back to the pound," she said. "With school and homework now you will not have time to take care of her." After a moment of shocked silence I began to wail. I could not have felt more pain if she had struck me with a sledgehammer. I could not comprehend that my puppy was gone for good. I had not been warned, I had not been prepared, I had not been consulted. They just took her away. My anguished howls of protest fell on deaf ears. Mom assumed I was upset in the way of a child denied an ice cream cone. She simply could not understand the depth of my emotional distress.

Inconsolable, I mourned Penny as if she had died. Was she okay? Did she think I abandoned her? Would she be well cared for? No one tried to console me, however. As far as my parents were concerned I had a dog, just like I always wanted. In some strange way they thought they'd done a good thing! Not so long ago I realized, with horror and fury, that they had never intended for me to keep that dog. They knew the day we got her that it would only be temporary.

One evening at dinner a few years later my father, in casual conversation, told Mom that a client of his, a veterinarian, was looking for part-time help. "I was thinking," he said with a surreptitious glance at me, "of maybe asking Danny or Jackie (my cousins)." I was at him like a rabid raccoon. "*What about me*?????" He grinned. He'd had me in mind all along. That Saturday morning we visited the office, where we were ushered into an exam room. There was the vet, with a Doberman on the table. Without hesitation I walked up to the dog and began to talk to him, scritching his ear. The doc asked when I could start. "Is there to be no interview?" my dad asked. "I've seen enough," the vet replied.

Back at home I burst through the door, anxious to share my excitement with my mother. She seemed oddly subdued. A day or so later, Dad came home from work with the news that my prospective employer had suffered an angina attack, and there would be no job for me. The truth, as I know it now, is that my dad had suffered a "Mom" attack. "SHE MIGHT GET BITTEN! SHE MIGHT GET A DISEASE!" This was no job for a lady, and my job was to be a lady. Once again, my mother had failed to understand her only child.

So Richard and I claimed Eric, my uncle's oversized red Doberman, as our proxy dog. He was something of a spoiled brat and not very well trained. One evening, lacking any formal plans, we decided to take him for a ride.

My uncle brought him out to the car, and he jumped in willingly. We drove to a large shopping mall which had recently opened and walked him right inside. Malls were still a novelty then, and dogs were allowed. He was a perfect gentleman, and we basked in the barrage of compliments he received.

When the mall closed we returned to the car, opened the door, and beckoned him in. He put on his brakes. We urged; he stiffened. We pushed; he growled. We pondered; he smirked. Clearly he had the upper hand. With apologies to Sacred Scripture, I would argue that it is easier to pass a camel through the eye of a needle than a reluctant Doberman anywhere he doesn't want to go. One thing was certain—I would not call my uncle and admit defeat! Finally I got an idea: I went around the car and opened the door on the other side. Richard threw the leash in, and I grabbed it and pulled as I called the dog. Richard shoved from the rear. Success! We brought him back, assuring his master that he'd behaved impeccably the whole evening. It was our secret, and the dog never told.

We had another mishap around the same time. Headed for the Forest Park Zoo on a Saturday morning, we happened to notice a synagogue across the street from the main entrance to the grounds. Weekly services were being held. Richard asked, "Do you mind?" and in we went. We were greeted in the vestibule by a senior member of the congregation, who welcomed us and introduced himself by name. Richard responded in kind and, as soon as he gave my name, the man recognized it as he knew my father. He graciously ushered us inside and found us seats. I caught a few funny glances but thought it was simply because I was obviously not Jewish. It didn't take me long to realize that people were staring because I wasn't a man! We had found an orthodox shul, where men pray separately from women, and I was the only female there. I stood out like a nudist in a Buddhist temple. To their credit, after a moment the worshipers returned to their prayers, and I sat back and let the calm sanctity of the atmosphere envelop me. It was an interesting experience, but one we did not repeat.

At the end of August Mary Anne and I revisited Cape Cod, this time with Richard and her then-boyfriend, John, along. It was so satisfying to be away from home and among strangers, where we could act like any other engaged couple, flashing my diamond and flaunting our status. We had a great weekend.

We continued dating throughout the fall when, to our amazement, my mother invited Richard to Thanksgiving dinner. She was a wreck, wanting to make a good impression; he was a wreck, wanting to make a good impression. The evening was an unqualified success, and Richard's place in the family was acknowledged. We were now "the four of us." In one comic moment my father, carving the turkey, asked Richard if he preferred breast or leg. Richard chose leg. I breathed a sigh of relief, having plenty of the latter and not so much of the former. My dad was talking about the bird, of course.

My father was about to steal some of our thunder with good news of his own. I was at Forbes and Wallace one day, happily drawing flow charts, when the office phone rang. It was the switchboard operator, who announced in a tremulous voice that the governor's office was on the line for me! My father had been appointed to a judgeship by then-governor Francis Sargent. He was in Boston that day for a confirmation hearing, and my mother had promised to call as soon as the proceedings ended. She was able to report good news: his nomination had been approved. The governor-called-Bette story spread through the store like wildfire, and I was quite a celebrity for a few days.

The elevator operator was another matter entirely. When Richard and I entered the car one day for a quick stop at my office on the eighth floor, he smiled and asked if we were brother and sister as we looked so much alike. Nothing unusual about that, we'd heard it before. The odd thing was, we were holding hands at the time! He seemed relieved when we assured him that we were not blood relatives.

FALSE PROMISES

Chapter
26

Not having had a lot of experience with weddings, and thinking the gesture was a made-for-the-movies gimmick, Richard was unnerved to learn that he would be expected to ask my father for my hand in marriage. Richard was more than a little in awe of this accomplished man and tried to weasel his way out of the assignment. I wouldn't let him off the hook. It was just *done*, and he'd have to do it. He picked a night and approached my dad with sober countenance and earnest demeanor. He stated his case simply, with conviction. My dad asked, "Do you love her?" That was easy. Richard answered "Yes, with all my heart." The next question was tricky: "How will you support her?" But Richard was ready with his reply. "I am going to be an attorney. Bette has a good job; I will work part-time and go to school. I will earn my law degree." And then the last test: "Are you very sure about this?" Again—easy: "YES!" While he did not exactly hand me over on a silver platter, my dad made it clear that he would not object and wished us well. I knew at that moment that my father, and therefore my mother, would be behind us every step of the way with their love and assistance.

Once both sides accepted the fact that this marriage was going take place, arrangements were made for our parents to meet. We would join them for dinner at a popular restaurant near my home. In an interesting role-reversal Richard was clean-shaven, attired in suit and tie, as was my dad. The bearded

Paul, on the other hand, still trying to hang on to his youth, wore bellbottoms and boots, with a Nehru jacket and large pendant on a heavy chain. The atmosphere was cordial as we ate, with serious discussion reserved until afterward, when tensions began to escalate. Aside from the religious issue, the matter of Richard's age needed to be addressed. A great deal hinged on the Isacoffs' willingness to allow Richard to wed at nineteen, as the legal age for a male to marry in Massachusetts was twenty-one. Without their consent there could be no wedding.

Painfully aware that Paul had total control in this delicate negotiation and that he knew it, too, we held our breath and clasped sweaty hands together under the table. All around us we could hear bits of animated conversation and occasional snorts of joyous laughter. Even though fellow diners were enjoying an ordinary evening with good friends, the air above our table was heavy with the weight of uncertainty. We had no reason to believe that Richard's parents would consent to this marriage, though why they would take an active role in his life now, after leaving him to his own devices all these years, was beyond me.

Chapter
27

Richard's earliest memories are of feelings rather than events: fear, loneliness, and anxiety. Any psychologist today would recognize depression, but it was not so readily diagnosed in the fifties. He has little recall of his childhood, but bears the impression of a chaotic home environment in which his father's anger often presented in impressive verbal tirades, and his mother repressed her emotions behind a facade of rigid control. It seemed as if the very house was yelling, with the television on so loud and its occupants screaming over the din.

At the same time though, TV was the young boy's refuge and solace. He would arise at 4:30 a.m. to peace and quiet while the others were asleep, and watch *Modern Farmer, Mr. Wizard, Sunrise Semester, Father Knows Best, The Real McCoys, December Bride* . . . almost anything including the test pattern, all day long, ad nauseam. Richard lived for, with, and through the television. It kept him from thinking about himself. More importantly, many of his values came from shows such as *Mr. District Attorney, The Defenders*, and *I Led Three Lives*, as well as from a reaction formation to his father's seemingly amoral behaviors. His most dreaded punishment was revocation of TV privileges.

Not only did he use the tube as a distraction, he had little else to do besides watch the shows. Worry occupied a lot of his time. As a youngster, he fretted incessantly about joining the Navy—no doubt a result of his father's experiences, related or intimated. Paul, having seen atomic devastation firsthand, was certain that nuclear war was imminent. His conviction was internalized by his impressionable son. By age thirteen, Richard was terrified of an impending World War III and developed an extreme fear of dying. He decided that he would live to be one hundred years old in an attempt to defend against his all-consuming panic. There was no one to help the frightened little boy. Richard was like Harlow's monkeys, who were nurtured with the wire-frame surrogate mother instead of the terry cloth one. Maybe Doris, who was ignored by her own father and cheated on by her husband, turned away from Richard before he could reject her too. His parents were preoccupied with keeping their own demons at bay, and his grandfather wouldn't have understood his every-day terror. Extended family members were no sounder emotionally: of the six cousins born to Doris and her sister, all suffered bouts of depression, or worse.

If the family drew straws to choose its scapegoat, Richard surely got the short one. He was not like his parents and the older of his two sisters, who fancied herself a Jewish American Princess and would even ask with great pride, "Don't I look Jappy?" In contrast to his group of buddies, Richard was not at all ethnic in his demeanor; he simply was himself. He was spiritual, if not particularly religious, and the rest of the family seemed to be neither. Richard felt close to Mindy, the youngest, but even she was more adventurous, and willing to experiment, than he. These differences set him apart from the others. They often ganged up against him, as dysfunctional families will, to blame him for problems real or imagined.

Richard brought all this heavy baggage with him to the playground. He sensed he was different from other kids and tended to keep to himself. Though he got along with his peers he was always one step to the side, not ahead or behind but on a parallel track. The tracks rarely converged. He met up with the others occasionally to play but was not part of any group. Behind his house appeared a huge dirt pile one summer that held his attention for many weeks. Sometimes a few neighborhood kids would join him there, and they might move on to a game of pirates, detectives, or cowboys and Indians. He has managed to remember mosquito spray trucks and one trip to visit Grandma Lena in Philly. The family stopped along the way to buy the kids presents: Richard got a toy carwash. He recalls no friend until he was already old enough to be riding a two-wheeler. He can recollect little from his early years, just snippets of activity overshadowed by unbearable sadness and pain.

One bright spot was summer camp, a Catholic day camp, which he attended from ages seven to twelve. Curiously, he remembers a lot about it and was relatively happy. Though he had only Jewish friends at home, of necessity he ran with a much more ecumenical crowd there. That was okay with him until prayer time, when mention was made of the Holy Ghost. *GHOST*??? The idea of a resident ghost was terrifying to him. The rest of the campers seemed to take it in stride, but Richard was ever on the lookout for this elusive spirit.

He held his camp experience separate from the rest of his life. It was a different world, one in which he felt he belonged. When he did have time to himself, he would go to the swamp just to think. About what, he can no longer say. The twelve-year-olds would advance to overnight camp but, sadly, Richard refused to go. His somewhat carefree days came to an end. Back home he distinguished himself academically, earning straight A's until seventh grade and excelling at math. Though he reverted to being a loner, alone, lonely, he didn't recognize it. He says, "I always had me. I was on my own, almost totally responsible for myself." Comfortably living in his head he would retreat into his private world, blocking out family, neighborhood, and other kids.

Perhaps because of Paul's pursuit of the hobby, Richard learned photography on a Nikon SP, a high-end camera back then. He knew more about processing film than the teacher who was faculty advisor to the school's camera club. The man would have killed for the camera he had.

Though father and son also had a mutual interest in firearms, their handling of weapons could not have been more different. When a dissatisfied customer returned a car radio to Yale Auto Parts, Paul simply took out a .44 Magnum and shot it! Richard became a marksman as a member of his junior high's rifle team, probably because of his expertise in photography. The techniques were the same. Block out the rest of the world; lose yourself in what you're doing; intense focus—gun or camera. 200 was a perfect score, and Richard regularly earned above 190. Later he would also excel at bicycle racing, another solitary sport where no one could get close to him. He would go as far as he could on his bike, riding for hours and hours. One summer he did about five miles every day to a store in Amity. He would buy a Tom Swift book each trip, until he'd read them all. Richard's fondest memories of this time were his stops at Naigel's Deli on the way home from bowling, where he would buy "a pickle for a nickel."

But Richard was not all innocence. Riding sidecar with the mysterious Holy Ghost was the devil himself, always willing to point out an opportunity for mischief. There was a neighbor, Mr. Gordon, who had the habit of confiscating errant softballs thrown in the direction of his house, which stood at right field. While the Gordons were on vacation, one player casually tossed a crab apple at their air conditioner. It stuck. HA! He threw some more; then all the others joined in. The appliance chewed up the wayward fruit and belched back applesauce. Though there was no damage done Mr. Gordon had to clean it, and his efforts provided the boys with an afternoon of entertainment.

One day, holding a plate as his intended target, Richard shot himself in the thumb with a pellet gun. Then there was the fire, started behind his house with David Rodman. It began as a hot dog roast but ended up toasting the property.

It makes you wonder if Richard did some of these things to cause trouble, or if he was trying desperately to attract his father's attention. Growing up, he worried constantly about pleasing Paul and winning his approval. The man had little to do with his only boy, and Richard felt that he didn't fit his father's image of what he wanted in a son. His question was, "Why?" As so many children do, he wanted to go to work with his dad when he was young. But Paul was not thrilled to bring him. If the boy was up and ready, okay. If not, Paul would slip out of the house alone. Several times Paul and a friend went scuba diving, and Richard was invited. Once on the boat, however, the men went about the business of having fun, and Richard was left to amuse himself. Then there was the remote-control airplane which Paul purchased for his son, but flew instead with a fellow service veteran.

Did Paul still see himself as the eternal playboy, not wanting to acknowledge or admit to fatherhood? The first time Richard went to the barber shop on his own, he announced excitedly to the man cutting his hair that he was Paul Isacoff's son. When he got home and proudly told his father, he got scolded. "Don't ever," Paul chastised, "tell anyone you're my son."

Because his father never taught him the requisite skills, Richard did not do well playing team sports. All of the other kids' fathers were jocks, some better than others, who engaged their sons in games of catch; supported them; encouraged them. Richard had to learn by himself. It may have been just as well, since other fathers taught by example, and Paul taught by ridicule. But Richard endured teasing at the playground anyway. The cool kids made fun of his big feet, calling him "wobbles." He did eventually play tackle football and softball, and was accepted into the Little League minors. Though he couldn't hit, he made a winning catch to beat the best team in the league. Of course, Paul was engaged elsewhere that day.

It took a hospital visit for Richard, with leg sliced open, to have Paul show up. Later, in junior high, when Richard was to receive several honors at his graduation awards ceremony, a favorite teacher personally called to ask his father to attend the event. She knew that he would be unlikely to appear otherwise. How sad it is that Richard was amazed to see him there.

Contrast Paul's lack of interest with my father's concern and support for this boy, whom he would come to love as his own son (I often teased, after we were married, that I had to remind my dad which of us was his real child and which was the in-law!). When Richard passed the bar exam to be licensed to practice law in Massachusetts, he was sworn in at the State House in Boston. My dad found a substitute judge to sit in his courtroom for the day, and my parents came with us to the ceremony. After the proceedings were over, dad proudly took Richard to meet the Chief Justice and other dignitaries; then treated us all to a lovely celebration dinner in Beantown. My father would not have missed this day for anything.

Around the age of thirteen, Richard was finally admitted to the magical world of Yale Auto Parts: he went to work for his father that summer. From the beginning, he could do nothing right. Paul would give him a task to do without details or explanation, then criticize the boy when he did it wrong. Once, Paul offered ten cents for every taillight lens he retrieved from cars in the yard. Energized and enthusiastic, Richard ran from vehicle to vehicle, snatching the glass from each. Proudly he brought back the lot and waited expectantly, eagerly, for his money. Instead, he got a reprimand. "I only wanted lenses from cars whose taillight assemblies were no good!" Paul ranted. "If the chrome and lightbulb socket were okay, I wanted you to leave the lens in place! I could have sold the assembly as an intact unit."

But this incident did not stop Paul from leaving Richard in charge of the business, at the tender age of sixteen, when he went to an auto parts dealers' conference for a few days. While he was away, an employee working on a car outdoors was injured due to his own carelessness. Richard was inside the building at the time and saw nothing of what happened. When Paul returned, he blamed Richard for the accident.

Cars and photography, boating and scuba diving, even gadgets—Richard embraced the hobbies and interests that Paul flirted with. Maybe his father would recognize the connection? But what if Richard turned out to be better at those activities? He offered everything he could, trying to develop a relationship with his father. No matter what Richard did, it could never be enough. Paul held the elusive carrot of approval ever farther ahead, as if in front of a famished donkey. "Be more like me!" he urged, in subtle yet unmistakable ways. Richard yearned for his father's approval. Yet, like any self-respecting donkey, he had a stubborn streak as well. He spurned the wanton lifestyle his father craved. Paul hoped to live vicariously through Richard, urging upon him the fast cars and fast women that he was expected to put aside. He did not want to see his son shackled with marital responsibilities. He couldn't help being disappointed in the boy who walked the straight and narrow, conservative in bearing and behavior.

When we went, with the Isacoffs, to a Jai Alai fronton for an evening's entertainment, Richard muttered, moaned and cheered as the action dictated, with dignity and restraint. Paul yelled, swore, and frequently jumped into the air, middle finger held aloft like the bayonet on which he would skewer the offending player, if only he could. What Richard didn't know was that, in turning away from that carrot in his youth, he was walking right past Rocky Road, Tutti Frutti and the sprinkles and heading for me . . . vanilla, pure and simple.

Richard's early fears of nuclear annihilation had not faded. The Cuban missile crisis of the early sixties heightened his terror, as did rumblings of war in Viet Nam. His was a "nowhere to run, nowhere to hide" mentality. In matters of international conflict, Richard and Paul were polar opposites. Paul was politically a right-winger but a social liberal; Richard embraced the same views socially. But he was not a hawk. He wanted no fighting any- where, ever. Paul's answer to the world's problems? "Nuke 'em!" Only he wasn't kidding. This overwhelming dread of global destruction, at the root of which was the thought of his own demise, pushed any motivation to excel in high school to the extreme fringes of Richard's consciousness. To him, these four years were about marking time until he could enter college. He did only what he had to do—no more, no less. A Latin teacher, Ann McGuff, seeing that he was adrift, tried to motivate and direct him in matters aca- demic and personal. Informing him that his IQ was in the genius range, she urged him to apply himself to his studies. "Don't waste your life!" she exhorted. Richard occupied himself, not with class assignments, but with camera club activities, audiovisual work, and the school newspaper. In spite of this, he was selected to represent Lee High at Connecticut Boys' State, a conference sponsored by the American Legion for training in civic leadership. He didn't care that his grades were mediocre. With high SAT scores he knew he would be accepted at a good college, later graduating magna cum laude. Rhoda Spear, whom he would have for various classes from seventh through twelfth grades, pushed him in the direction of Clark University in Worcester, sent glowing letters of recommendation, and noted with satisfaction that her prize student was offered a place in the Class of 1972.

Chapter
28

As he evolved from boy to man, Richard's dream was to pursue a career in either law or journalism/photojournalism. He was particularly drawn to constitutional law and investigative work. Regardless of the path he chose to follow, it would lead to the pursuit of justice for all people. He wanted to protect and ensure the rights of the average person and considered aiming for a US Senate seat. What better way is there to affect the way laws are made than to be there making them? Richard naïvely believed in the system and wanted to change it from within to make it better. He saw only right or wrong and believed that Senators always did what was right. With his purist mind-set he sincerely felt that he would work hard for the people, not recognizing the wheeling and dealing, the compromise that is politics.

Richard had never been in the system and didn't know how it worked. My dad, a political operative and heavyweight in the Republican Party, did know but refused to go along. True, my father was a Judge, but the road to the bench had been rocky. Initially he was nominated by Governor John Volpe, with confirmation to come after an interview with the Governor's Council. There was another individual who wanted the judgeship badly. My father received a call from one member of the Council: "You are undoubtedly the more qualified candidate. However, we have been offered a substantial sum of money (the amount was specified) from the other party. If you will only match his offer, the judgeship is yours." Without hesitation, my father turned him down. It so happened that the Governor was stricken with what was believed to be a heart attack, and my dad got another call. "We will not go against the wishes of a dying man," he was told. "Come to Boston for the formality of an interview, and the judgeship is yours."

When he arrived at the meeting, Dad learned that the Governor's near-fatal episode turned out to be only indigestion. The previous offer was reinstated: pay up and we'll vote you in. He left the room in disgust. Years later, when Governor Francis Sargent called to offer a nomination, my dad told him straight out, "I will not spend a dime to buy anyone a cup of coffee for this judgeship. Know that right now." The Governor did know, which is one reason he tapped my father for the job. The confirmation went through without a hiccup.

"Justice," the concept and its pursuit, consumed Richard. If he wrote an article for the school paper, it was usually to expose some injustice. Remember the school riots, when the police tried to confiscate his film? His cleverness in preventing them from getting their hands on it was not so much about having the pictures as it was about fairness. He felt strongly that they had no right to take it. And the incident with the school keys, where he faced the administration and backed them down? Again, Richard instinctively upheld fairness. It was *his* camera that had been stolen along with the tuba, and they were trying to accuse *him* of theft? He was proud of himself for taking a stand.

Others recognized his commitment to justice for all. When he ran for Senior Council, his campaign was endorsed by the leader of the Black kids at the school. How like my father he was! There was a time during the racial upheavals of the sixties that the Black community in Springfield demanded a Black officer in every patrol car (a step up from walking the beat). At the time Dad, still an attorney, was Chairman of the Police Commission, so it became his issue to resolve. Refusing to bend under pressure, he outlined the procedure for promotion, to be accorded to each man equally based only on merit. He thought the matter was settled. Returning from Court one afternoon, he entered his reception area to find his secretary shaking in her chair, her face frozen with fear. Remember—racial tensions were rampant then. With her sat a delegation of Black men waiting to see my father. He invited them into his office, not knowing what to expect. The leader began to speak. "We are here," he said, "to ask you to run for Mayor." Honored, my father asked why. "You may not always give us what we want," the man continued, "but we know you will treat us fairly. We cannot ask for more than that." Thanking them for their confidence in him he respectfully declined, having no interest in the position.

Richard lived what he preached. At a time when an evening's entertainment for many of his classmates consisted of marijuana parties or crossing the line into New York to get drunk, he did neither. Still depressed, still basically a loner, he continued to grow apart from the other kids. Not liking what they did, he was not upset that he didn't fit in. He wasn't having sex like most of them were. He dated rarely, and today remembers the names of only two girls he saw. He never cared for The (early) Beatles. He did not drink or smoke . . . anything. In fact, he and Stuart worked with a police informant, Tommy, then in his early twenties. When one of the school kids dealing drugs needed to go to New York to make a buy, Tommy set up a sting. Stuart would drive, with Richard accompanying. My boys stayed in the car, having nothing to do with the purchase. On the way back, with the transaction complete, they signaled at a certain toll both that the deal had gone down. The police, waiting, arrested the perpetrator on the spot.

Richard's railings against social and political injustice were an acceptable outlet for his anger, born of the depression which continued unabated into his teens. He maintained tight control over this rage, and I only saw it expressed twice. Once, as we idled in Manhattan traffic, he kicked out of the car a stereo speaker that was mounted on the floor next to the door. Another time, he snapped a key in half. Everything was kept under wraps, yet there was that rare chink in his armor. When he left home to attend college, the physical distance from his family gave him the perspective to analyze the events of his life, and he started to understand their relevance to his injured psyche. With this insight, he would begin to heal.

But for now, not knowing that other families were different from his, he believed his own to be normal and saw himself as the odd one. He formed a loose association with my boys, themselves a group of social aliens. There were peripheral people in his life like David Shindell, a bookish boy who was probably the only true friend Richard ever had. David would be there to see us married. Bryan Rosner, whose parents were friends with the Isacoffs, hung out with Richard at the Colony Beach Club, an interesting venue populated almost exclusively by Jews and Italians.

Chapter
29

The day we met at Lee High School, though I wish I could say otherwise, Richard was as unimpressed with me as I was with him. The boys had to drag him to my dorm at Albertus for Open House that Sunday. I was their friend, not his. He had nothing else to do, so he came along. The first thing he observed, he tells me now, was simply that I was nice to him. He acknowledged to himself that, in spite of the fact that I had no motive, I was paying attention to him. Although he considered himself disposable, I didn't dispose of him. He noticed, and appreciated, that I differentiated him from the rest of the boys. Of course he would claim that, absenting himself from their nefarious escapades, he didn't even fit in with the misfits! Richard does not remember today how he felt then; his memories are reconstructions at best. He cannot even recall being at his law school graduation nine years later.

Richard was nothing if not proper. He knew that I went to a school where "proper" was stressed, as we even had to have suits and hats for tea. Eager to exhibit correct behavior, he jumped to open doors for me, stood aside for me to enter, and pulled out my chair in restaurants. In fact, he still does! The antithesis of his father, he set himself to learning how to be a considerate adult. While Paul prided himself on his lack of consideration for others. Uppermost in Richard's seventeen-year-old mind, in the matter of courting someone, was how to show good taste and class. But *this* someone was a twenty-one year old college senior.

He never gave his parents' reactions a thought. They had expressed so little interest in his life that he believed any impediments would be irrelevant. Given his philosophy of "people are people," the difference in our religions didn't matter to him. Since I had Jewish friends, he assumed it wouldn't matter to me. He didn't consider what it might mean to either set of parents.

Whereas Paul had a habit of being rude to people so as not to be rejected—an "I'll get you first" mentality—Richard tended to have nothing to do with people. He was willing to be shut out to protect himself from the sting of being judged. Yet he saw that we seemed to have an easy camaraderie, enjoyed each other's company, and had quite a bit in common. Though he did not think he would be, he decided to take the chance of being cast aside. "You were beautiful," he recalls, "and smart and funny." Most important of all, he trusted me. He felt secure and valued.

Richard dragged himself frog-like, muddied and bloodied, from the emotional swamp of his childhood. He emerged wide-eyed and unblinking, looking for approval. Raised like a cherished princess, I grew up with the acceptance he never had. I saw only good in him, and he began to see himself through my eyes. At last he'd found a safe haven where he could be himself. He dared to open his heart to me. Richard would be my frog prince.

Chapter
30

So here we were, all six of us—parents and betrothed—at a restaurant two years later, waiting for Paul's permission to wed. He held our fate in his hands. Curious that the man who had so little input in his son's life should now choose to exert parental authority. Just how late can you come to the party? Richard had made an independent decision, had chosen his own course, and now there was panic in the streets. He had been ignored for years and he went away like they wanted . . . now this.

Diplomatically my father tiptoed around the state statute, hoping that Paul would cooperate in facilitating our preparations. Though the ultimate decision was Paul's, he was up against a master negotiator. My father presented a strong case, and he eventually acquiesced, promising: "If it's a signature you want, I'll sign." He made it clear that although he was not happy, he would not stand in our way.

Having held her emotions in check for most of the evening, Doris suddenly rose from her chair and flounced off rather dramatically to the ladies' room, dabbing affectedly at her tear-filled eyes. Uncomfortable with confrontation and unable to express her thoughts directly, she embraced the victim role enthusiastically and performed it flawlessly. Concerned, and unaware of her theatrical flair, my mother got up to follow her. A quick glance from me told Mom to stay put. Within minutes Doris returned, subdued, to the table. She allowed herself a few dying-swan sniffles, looked about for a reaction and, seeing none, settled into her seat. Her performance was so contrived that the swan would have been embarrassed. Within minutes her cigarette puffs thickened the air, enveloping us like a shroud. (Or maybe it was residue from the ashes of her dreams going up in smoke.)

With formal talks concluded, the conversation turned to usual wedding topics like food, flowers, and music. Doris asked where the wedding would take place but, as she was unfamiliar with the area, our response would mean nothing to her. My father volunteered to detour past the reception site on our way back to the house so that she could see it firsthand. Though we could not know it at the time, her innocent question and his well-intentioned offer were the first step in the inexorable march toward the real wedding conflict to come.

But that night we were ignorant of the impending nightmare and excitedly led the party out to the car for the ride to the impressive venue. Upon seeing it Doris seemed satisfied, and Richard and I were able to relax at last. We were going to have a glorious wedding!

Chapter
31

With Paul's signature assured, we started planning our nuptials. Although I belonged to a different parish we chose to be wed at Mt. Carmel, especially since Richard was familiar with the church and would be more comfortable there. We made a visit to Father Santini, the pastor. We had two questions: would he be willing to preside at my marriage to a Jewish man, and would he consent to the presence of a rabbi at the service?

Reading this now, you may wonder what the big deal was. Intermarriage today is common and generally accepted, but it was not the situation in the sixties. Then, Catholics were required to marry other Catholics. On rare occasions permission would be given for marriage to a Protestant but never, ever to an unbaptized, or non-Christian, person. I was in the eighth grade when my cousin Cathy married an Episcopalian, as close to Catholic as you can get except that they don't view the Pope in quite the same way we do. The couple were not permitted onto the altar, as was customary for Catholic weddings, but were made to say their vows outside the altar rail. They were not allowed to have the traditional Nuptial Mass. The aura of disapproval was palpable. It was a bold, daring, and very determined Catholic that would challenge the "we only marry our own" rule. Yet here we were, a mere ten years later, asking the priest to sanction, and participate in, my marriage to someone who was once considered a non-believer.

To be fair, Jews at the time were equally exclusive about their offsprings' choices of marital bed-mates. While both religious groups took the "you'll find someone else to love" approach—much like a dog will bond with a new master, I suppose—I subscribed to the each-person-has-one-perfect-match theory. Richard was mine, and I was his.

We needn't have worried. This wonderful man would be delighted to marry us, and as for the rabbi? "Have him call me," he said, "and we'll work something out together." Not only could the rabbi stand as a witness, he would also participate equally with the priest. It would be an elegant, formal evening wedding on the eighth of August.

Richard and I were in charge of the ceremony, and my mother would handle the reception. I wanted the usual: flowers, candles, and music. I would depart from most of the traditional pieces common to such occasions in favor of more esoteric classical selections—and no Wagner bridal march! Instead of a soloist, I would ask that my beloved choir sing, with principal organist and good friend Mary Mastroianni at the keyboard. Everything would be arranged according to the strictest protocol.

Within hours of our return from the session with Fr. Santini, my mother had reserved the site for our party. Soon after, she lined up the wedding photographer, hired the limos, and was interviewing musicians. There would be no bunny hop! No alley cat (the barnyard repertoire had not yet expanded to include the chicken dance)! And no raising us up on chairs! She also arranged a sitting for me with Bradford Bachrach Studios for my engagement photo.

We went together, my mother and I, to look at wedding gowns. I knew what I wanted: long and white, classic and simple, without sequins, stones, beads, pearls, or lace. Though I was in a "money-is-no-object-it's-my-wedding-dress" frame of mind, we went first to Forbes & Wallace. Remember—employee discount! I knew when I saw it that this was the one: empire style with high neck; puffed sleeves, short with a wide band just above the elbow; skirt not full but not straight either, with a chapel train.

The only ornamentation on the dress was rows of white cotton embroidered flowers, spaced a few inches apart and running the length of the gown. The headpiece I selected was shaped, I hate to say, like a small Cool Whip container, and was covered with tiny flowers matching those of the dress. It featured a long veil. I would carry a Lily of the Valley bouquet, as my mother had done for her August 5th wedding many years earlier. What I would not wear was the traditional garter. I chose instead Bermuda Blue, the perfume of that island, for my "something blue."

Another day, we went shopping for dresses for my bridal party. I had designated Mary Anne Sullivan as maid of honor and two of my cousins as bridesmaids. Although I had not asked them yet, I hoped that Richard's two sisters would participate as well. Again I had specific requirements where these styles were concerned: above all, they were not to look bridesmaid-y! We were fortunate to find simple, square-necked, long-sleeved gowns in a very soft pink, with the palest green sash the only accent. Though difficult to describe, they were lovely. All of my attendants had long hair, which they would wear down, with the top pulled back and caught up with matching ribbon. They would be dressed identically. No rainbow colors or other contrivances for my wedding! Outfitting the men was easy. They would be in tails.

I made one more purchase, this time alone. Despite the fact that they are often given as shower gifts, I wanted to select personally the lingerie that I would wear on my wedding night. Peignoir sets were de rigueur then, consisting of nightgown and matching coat. Some were long, some were short, but there were no minis. More chaste and tasteful than sexy and provocative, most had yards of lace, ruffles, designs, or all three. To my great delight I found a lovely ensemble, soft and delicate. Sleeveless, the gown was empire in style, with a bodice made of the tiniest pleats. The skirt was plain, and there was minimal soft, delicate, lace edging the sleeves, neck, and skirt; it surrounded the bodice as well. Long-sleeved, with wide cuffs, the entire coat featured the same minuscule pleats with matching lace trim. I anticipated the thrill of wearing it as Richard's new bride.

Richard and I went together to order wedding bands, which we matched to my engagement ring. Inside each would be engraved "For as long as we live." This would also be our matrimonial promise to each other. Our commitment would not end with the death of either of us as it would be a marriage of souls, not just physical bodies. For as long as we might exist, in whatever dimension, our union would continue. At the jewelry store we also found an antique silver wedding cup, which we would use in lieu of the more common champagne glasses for the best man's toast to the bridal couple.

As soon as the proofs were ready, I returned to Bachrach to select a print for submission, with our engagement announcement, to newspapers in Springfield and New Haven. At the time, brides from prominent families were featured in the Sunday edition society pages. That year, Valentine's Day happened to fall on a Sunday, and we thought—why not? We sent the material to *The Springfield Sunday Republican* and *The New Haven Register* with a specific request for a February 14th release date.

We set about the task of finding a rabbi who would be willing to participate in a Catholic wedding service. Richard dismissed the head of his shul as a potential candidate at once, and we wondered where to turn next when the answer came to me. A rabbi in a town outside of Springfield was a member of the theology department at Albertus! I had never taken a class with him but I felt that, if he was progressive enough to teach religious studies at a Catholic college, he might be open to our request.

Sitting in his office, we presented our case for his consideration. It took him no time at all to reply. "You must break off this engagement. Jews are assimilating at an alarming rate. Every time someone marries out the community is weakened, and the very existence of the Jewish people is threatened. We must rebuild after the decimation of the Holocaust. You have a responsibility to contribute by making a Jewish home and raising Jewish children."

The rabbi had placed the survival of an entire ethnic group on the shoulders of one young man, whose personal happiness was of no consequence whatsoever. It would have been preferable for him to marry a Jewish girl whom he did not love! Richard was enraged, and I was devastated. But God, sticking to His agenda, pulled rank on the rabbi. Widening our search, we found a reform synagogue in southern Connecticut whose leader was willing to entertain the notion of a joint service, even if he had a bit of a hang-up about doing it in church. We left feeling that there was room for negotiation on that point. But disaster was just around the corner, and it had nothing to do with a rabbi.

All allotted space in the Valentine's Day issue of *The New Haven Register* had been reserved and, unknown to us as we were living in Massachusetts, the newspaper staff published the announcement one week early. Though I was still blissfully unaware, my wedding plans died that day.

FALSE EXPECTIONS

Chapter
32

Now that the news of our upcoming marriage would soon be public, Richard could no longer put off what he had most dreaded. He had to tell his grandfather in person. As nervous as Richard had been about a possible showdown with his mother and father, he was positively petrified of broaching the topic with his grandfather. So Harry had not the faintest idea that we were planning to wed. You can be certain that Doris had not brought this controversial tidbit of information to her father! Until the very last minute, she would hold on to a desperate hope that our relationship would end.

Harry came from a heritage of rabbis. Though not a rabbi himself, he had a strong commitment to his Jewish faith. Harry would be devastated to learn that Richard planned to wed outside the Jewish religion. In fact, fairly recently a nephew of his second wife had married a Protestant, and the family sat shiva as if he were dead. I wondered if Richard would be able to handle the guilt that would surely follow Harry's tears and pleadings. No doubt disappointed, Harry may have felt that a strenuous objection would drive Richard straight into my arms. After all, the deed was not done yet. Given time and space, Richard might still come to his senses and see the error of his ways. And so he simply asked, "Does she make you happy?" Religious issues aside, I believe that Harry understood the love in his cherished grandson's heart. Remember, his own two marriages had been arranged.

Lacking the nerve, Richard had not yet told his parents that our announcement would be appearing in the newspaper. He thought that he still had a week to summon up his courage. Their shock upon seeing my picture was bad enough, but then they read the article. Family phoned, friends called, busybodies put their two cents' worth in. "He's getting married at nineteen? To a *Catholic* girl? *In church, yet?*"

Even worse, Harry's business partner called him. Morris, not knowing that he didn't know about the announcement, was full of questions to which Harry had no answers. Harry in turn called Doris, and it was confusion and consternation all around.

We were not off the hook. In fact, we were impaled on it. I refer you back to the night our parents met for dinner, and Doris asked where the wedding would be held. She meant the ceremony! As one church looks pretty much like another, it never occurred to any of us that she would want to see Mt. Carmel. We all assumed she meant where would the reception take place, and that is what we showed her. At the time she was satisfied, thinking that we would be married on neutral territory. The misunderstanding came to light when she read, with no forewarning, that we would exchange our vows in a Catholic church. Furious, she demanded an explanation.

I thought I had a pretty convincing argument. By tradition, weddings are held at the church or synagogue of the bride. Further, we were regular churchgoers, and I was particularly active in that parish. Why should I marry in a synagogue, which the Isacoffs themselves rarely attended? Having the ceremony at the reception site, which is what Doris had anticipated, was out of the question. Richard and I both wanted the atmosphere of our wedding to be sacred, not profane. I could not accept the idea of some half-rate musician playing *Here Comes the Bride* on a plinky-plink piano in the lounge as Dad and I, doing the hesitation step so popular with brides then, promenaded toward my groom.

Initially Paul was pretty low-key about the whole thing, but Doris eventually wore him down with her anxiety and apprehension. He finally dug in his heels and delivered the devastating blow: neither Richard's parents nor any family members or friends would attend our wedding. Dumbstruck, Richard tried in vain to change their minds. After all, there would be a rabbi at the service—surely that made it all right? No, it didn't. We were in a quandary. Because of my father's associations, we expected some high-ranking political dignitaries and other prominent attendees at our celebration. There could be no hint of scandal or anything amiss. Further, Paul was no longer willing to sign for Richard to get married at all!

We went to see his parents together, to plead our case. His mother was her usual nervous self, flitting about from one topic to another, never giving us a concrete reason for her decision. "You're too young, she's not Jewish, the wedding is in church, your grandfather will have a heart attack (she was as concerned about Harry as my mother had been about her father) . . . ." Paul laughed and joked as if this were the funniest situation in the world. "Why don't you elope?" he teased. "You can rent a bus and we'll all go to Maryland." It wasn't funny, but very heartless and cruel. We walked out.

Back in Springfield, we told my parents what had happened. They kindly offered to go to New Haven themselves, to speak with the Isacoffs face-to-face. Calmly and reasonably, they presented their point of view. "Bette is our only child," they said. "Even though we were against this marriage, we would never turn our backs on her. We intend to be there for our daughter. Don't you feel the same about your only son?" It was a waste of time and effort. Once again Paul, knowing he had control of the situation, enjoyed himself immensely as he casually and carelessly trampled our plans, hopes, and dreams. My mom and dad left, frustrated and disappointed, having gotten nowhere. When they got home they related the conversation to us, with apologies for having failed. We thanked them for their efforts and assured them that they could not have done more. I went off to grieve by myself, mourning the loss of my special day. I understood that there would be no last-minute reprieve, no eleventh-hour miracle. There would be no wedding.

Chapter
33

Once we were certain that Richard's parents would not move from their position, we needed to reformulate our plans. We began to appreciate the serious consequences their stubborn refusal to participate in our wedding would have. First, the obvious: no signature meant no marriage. Even if we could find a way around that, without his relatives and their friends one side of the church would be empty. They would be noticeably absent from the reception as well. Questions would naturally be asked, and explanations would be expected. The situation was bound to take center stage, creating a major distraction from the solemn and joyous aspects of the day. Not wishing to commit a social faux pas which would cause my parents no end of embarrassment and distress, and compromise their standing in the community, we reluctantly and tearfully decided to cancel the August wedding. Doris and Paul had callously destroyed our dreams, but not our determination. We would say our vows, in simplicity rather than splendor, with or without their blessing. If my mother had any doubts about my love for Richard, they were dispelled when she realized that I was willing to forego my Cinderella fantasy in order to marry him.

As the end of Richard's sophomore year at Clark approached, we contemplated his housing options for the school vacation. He would have to find an apartment, as three months at home would have been unthinkable under the circumstances. I was living with my family for a reasonable monthly fee. Each of us had a car. We realized that duplicate rent payments and auto expenses were both wasteful and unnecessary and tried our best to come up with an alternative. Financial feasibility was a huge concern, since we were trying to save money for our new life as a couple. It hadn't occurred to us yet that, with all of the formal plans rescinded, we were no longer tied to the August date. We would need to downscale our wedding, but we did not have to wait. I don't remember which of us finally realized that we were free to make other arrangements. We could marry as soon as Richard finished the semester and spend the summer together with one car and one rent.

We sped off excitedly in this new direction, only to hit a major obstacle almost at once. Richard was still two years too young for marriage by Massachusetts standards. Securing the necessary parental signature was now out of the question, but we were undaunted. Richard began to search for a nearby state without the age restriction and was successful almost immediately. I would become his wife in Delaware. Since we had no ties to the area, he called the Wilmington Chamber of Commerce and requested the telephone number of a Catholic church—preferably an Italian parish. A kind priest answered his call and agreed to meet with us to determine our readiness for marriage. If we passed his scrutiny, he would be willing to perform the ceremony. He asked that we bring with us a letter of endorsement from my home parish, St. Stanislaus, along with my baptismal certificate.

In the Catholic Church, permission was required to wed outside one's parish, whether in a chapel right next door or a cathedral hundreds of miles away. Months before, we had gotten the okay from my church for Fr. Santini to marry us at Mt. Carmel, so we knew that the religious difference was no impediment to consent. The need for parental sanction would be circumvented by our marrying out of state, so we could foresee no objection to our request. We scheduled a brief appointment at the rectory, anticipating no problem in getting the necessary approval.

Ah, but this is our story, so of course there was a problem. When we arrived for our meeting, the good Father stiffly informed us that he would have to deny permission. Being a Massachusetts church, St. Stan's was bound by Commonwealth law. The priest had to hold us to local requirements even though Delaware regulations were different, meaning that Richard's parents could still prevent our marriage. It must have been Divine intervention that inspired my reply. I let my facial features sag lower than a Basset Hound's and, looking as pathetic as could be, lamented the fact that I would not have a church wedding.

Forty-something years ago, anything other than an exchange of vows at a Catholic altar was anathema to persons of my faith. For good measure I added that, if we could not marry in the Delaware church, we would be forced to seek the services of a Justice of the Peace for a civil service here in Massachusetts. To his credit as a man of God, the priest considered his contribution to my soul's eternal damnation if he forced me to marry outside the Church, relented at once, and agreed to write the letter. Had he not felt the weight of my salvation so heavy on his shoulders, it might have occurred to him that a local JP would be bound by the same state regulations. He would not be able to marry us either! But in fact he did not think of it at the time, and we left his company with the priceless document in our possession.

We bounded into my house, ecstatically waving the letter at my mom. She rejoiced with us for a moment and then sat at the kitchen table, thoughtful and serious. "You need to tell your mother," she said to Richard. Ever the peacemaker, she felt that Doris should know about her son's upcoming marriage and have the chance to attend the wedding. We had not intended to call New Haven, but there would be no refusing. A volley of excuses did nothing to sway Mom. She stood firm. Richard was not bending either. Finally, she suggested that a mother-to-mother talk might actually be the best course, and we heartily agreed. As we stood by, she placed the call.

Doris answered the phone, and after an exchange of pleasantries my mom got down to business. "I overheard the kids talking," she began, "and it appears that they are driving to Delaware to get married! I am not any happier about this union than you are, but Bette is my only child. If she is going to marry I certainly want to be there, and I thought I would let you know so that you could be, too. They have said that if they go away without our support they will not come back."

With a laugh Doris replied, "They're not going anywhere. They have no money. How would they live? Don't worry, they'll be back!" And that was the end of the conversation. Mom shrugged. She had done her best. Her heart went out to Richard, who was disappointed and hurt by his mother's cavalier attitude. Did she have no soul? Could she not see the pain she was causing? Didn't she care? It was all about *her*, and never mind the cost to her only son, and to me.

Wait a minute . . . a little specter of guilt danced its way into brain cells long ago decommissioned and consigned to storage. Why was I feeling squirmy, as if the shamefulness of her attitude was trying to attach itself to me? It felt like I'd been there before.

And then, I knew. The worms; the frogs. How could I have been so callous? Was I sensitive to their suffering? Privy to *their* pain? The truth is, it never occurred to me to consider their stake in my experiments. It was all about *me*—I'd had no more concern for the consequences of my behavior than Doris now had for hers. It was not until I became a victim myself that I understood the enormity of what I had done, putting my own interests above those of healthy, thriving creatures who had as much right to their place on this earth as I did.

I had played God with living beings, and now Doris was playing God with us. Granted, my parents had given it their best shot too, but at least ultimately they did have my welfare at heart and sacrificed their dream of what my marriage would be so I could pursue mine.

We began to formulate travel plans that would include my parents, but not his. My godmother, to whom I had always been close, would also be making the trip. With a heavy heart, Mom called all those to whom she had sent deposits for services to advise them that there would be no party. No refunds were forthcoming.

Richard contacted the DuPont, the grandest hotel in Wilmington, and asked to reserve the bridal suite. They had a presidential suite, a gubernatorial suite . . . everything but. Richard said, "I'll take the best you have."

Sympathetic but practical, my mother suggested that I cancel the order for my wedding dress. After all, we would not be having a wedding, but just a simple service with a few people present. That's where I drew the line. I was willing to give up a lot. Bucking the burgeoning feminist trend, I even happily turned in my maiden name to assume Richard's surname. (Isn't a man's name one of the most treasured gifts he can give to a woman?) But I would be a bride, with all that it entailed. The order stood.

I still wanted Richard in tails, too. We pruned the wedding party to just the maid of honor and best man. Fortunately, the attendants' dresses had not been purchased yet. Mary Anne would wear her own frock—a lovely gown of soft blue; John a dark suit, white shirt, and tie.

One discussion I never had with my mother was the wedding night talk, still fairly common in the 1960s. It's not that I was so knowledgeable, but she would have preferred to walk through fire than talk about that. Much later she would tell me that, as a young woman, she was disgusted with her father, who had actually "done it" twelve times! She had eleven siblings. Imagine her chagrin when she realized that he had probably done it ever so much more.

Richard, on the other hand, got unsolicited advice from each parent. His father urged him to get lots of sexual experience with different women before he settled down with a wife; his mother warned him not to marry a virgin. Well, he didn't, and he did. Our marriage, and our sexual relationship, would be exclusive and special.

TRUE LOVE

Chapter
34

On Monday, the 27th of April, Richard and I drove to Wilmington to make arrangements for the wedding. We visited Fr. Roberto Balducelli, the priest who had so kindly agreed to marry us. Convinced at once of our sincerity and resolve, he took us through a quick rehearsal. Then we left for City Hall to procure a marriage license. Two more stops, to order flowers (there would be no Lily of the Valley bouquet: they would have been in season for my August wedding, but were not available in May) and a cake, and we were on our way home.

We were not out of the woods. In fact, Richard almost ended up in the jungle! Because of the Vietnam War, a new draft lottery was instituted that year. A few weeks earlier, on the eve of the drawing, Richard strutted about the campus, confident that his number would somehow be missed (draftees would be chosen by their birth dates). The following day, he chuckled as he saw a student parading around with a huge "007" on his chest. The unfortunate fellow had come up number seven out of a possible 365—a guaranteed ticket to basic training. Uncharitably perhaps, Richard thought "Better you than me, buddy!" Later that day he learned that his birth date, September 7th, was number eight! Truly opposed to killing (without any hippie connotations), he could not see himself as an active participant in this conflict.

He made the decision to join the Massachusetts National Guard in an effort to avoid being sent to Viet Nam.

Although males across the Commonwealth were flocking to local recruiting offices, Richard went to the top. He called MNG headquarters in Boston. After being shuffled around a bit, he was finally put in touch with a colonel. He explained that he was a college student in Worcester, and would like to sign up. "Where do you live?" the colonel asked. Well...Worcester, of course! "Yes, but where do you *live?*" he persisted. Richard was from Connecticut, he admitted, BUT he would soon be marrying a Massachusetts native and taking up residence here. He stated that, while he was more than willing to serve his country, he was not a fighter and could not picture himself in armed combat. Additionally, having turned down appointments to two of the service academies (West Point and Air Force), he feared the military would extract its revenge!

The colonel chuckled at this and advised Richard that there was just one spot open for an inductee. "You won't want to be driving to Boston all the time for drills," the colonel said, "so call Lou Thibideau in Springfield." He was actually at Battalion Headquarters in Westfield. "You can use my name." With profuse thanks, Richard hung up and immediately dialed the local number. He was told to come to Westfield and enlist. He joined on the 29th of April. (Eventually, he would become MNG's senior photographer.)

That same night, my bridal shower was held. When our wedding plans changed so abruptly, the four sisters (my aunts Mary, Charlotte, Alice, and Susie) had scrambled to plan a lovely party for me. Even with short notice, many women attended. I wore a Victor Joris ensemble, of course. The evening was a huge success, but I couldn't help wondering if some were attributing the new wedding date to an unexpected pregnancy! They'd learn the truth soon enough, when no baby came.

Early Friday morning, we left for Delaware. My parents picked up Mary Anne and followed us several hours later. We visited the florist and bakery for a quick preview (Richard would go back for the flowers and cake, and buy champagne, in the morning). When everyone had arrived at Howard Johnson's, where we would be staying, we all went out for a festive dinner and then returned to the motel. I remember relaxing with Richard on one of the beds in the room Mary Anne and I would share this last night. For a quarter it would vibrate —a novelty at that time—and we decided to give it a try. My mother hovered nearby, worried even then that her daughter's innocence might be compromised. There were about a half-dozen people in the room. What were the chances? Even so, she was ever my diligent protector. By 10:00 p.m. only Mary Anne and I remained, and we had a whispered conversation in the dark before she dropped off to sleep. I stayed awake a while longer, shivering with anticipation and watching the clock as the waning minutes of my girlhood ticked away.

The second of May, 1970, dawned as a gloriously perfect spring day, but I was up before the sun. I fussed with my hair and makeup and tried to pacify the butterflies in my stomach. My jitters were not from nerves, but from overwhelming elation. I went to the church with my parents and Mary Anne while Richard and John, Mary Anne's boyfriend and Richard's best man, rode together.

Besides the wedding party, priest, server, and organist, there would be eight people at our service. In addition to my mom and dad, my family was represented that day by my aunt Alice, her husband Pete, and their son, Jay. Richard's support system consisted of two college friends and David, his boyhood pal from New Haven. I thought briefly about the wedding that might have been, but my great joy was in no way diminished by the unfortunate turn of events.

My dad and I stood in the vestibule of the church, waiting for the music that would cue us to begin our processional. Mary Anne preceded us, to the strains of a pleasing classical piece with a melody I do not remember and a name I cannot recall. Then I heard the telltale first bars of Wagner, and nearly turned and ran. I had always been determined to avoid the plebeian *Here Comes the Bride* at all costs. In the rush to finalize arrangements on

Monday, I had neglected to specify any particular musical selections to the organist. I was quickly able to laugh it off, adding this to the ever-lengthening string of mishaps surrounding these nuptials. All was forgotten as I approached the altar and saw the deep love and great happiness in Richard's heart reflected in his beautiful, soft green eyes.

We had the distinction of being married twice in the same ceremony. When we came to the exchanging of rings, Richard nervously quoted the priest as he placed the wedding band on the wrong finger. Smiling, the priest asked that he remove the ring and try again. He got it right, and we led the recessional outside into the brilliant sunshine. Married at last!

Upon leaving the church, the guests made their way to our hotel suite for a small but joyous celebration. We trusted that they would understand our penurious circumstances and forgive the limited wedding fare of cake and champagne. While we settled in, my dad went to retrieve our luggage from the car. As we gratefully acknowledged the compliments and congratulations, a small corner of my mind registered the fact that my father had been gone longer than necessary. When he finally returned, he invited the ensemble to follow him to a lovely private dining room, where we enjoyed an elegant filet mignon dinner with waiter in attendance, starched linen towel folded over his flexed arm. It was a loving and thoughtful gesture, a father's first gift to his newly-married daughter.

Surprised and sated, we went back to the suite for the opening of gifts and a toast to the bridal couple. Richard first stomped a napkin-wrapped glass in deference to his Jewish background. We removed the wedding cake from its box and set it on a small table. Although in the 1970s most confections were topped by traditional bride-and-groom figurines, I had chosen instead a simple, white, gardenia-like icing flower. As my maid of honor deftly presented the gifts and then arranged them for display, her heel hooked a stray bow whose ribbon was wrapped around a chair leg. She stumbled toward my dainty wedding cake, flattening the sugary blossom with a deep elbow imprint. She was unharmed, and after a good laugh we cut the cake, its taste unaffected by its shape. All photos in which the cake appear were shot from a considerable distance.

The trip from Delaware to New England takes several hours, and our guests began to say their goodbyes. Before my parents left, they urged Richard to phone his family with the news. Reluctantly, as he knew the reaction would not be favorable, he placed the call. Mindy answered. Not wanting to provoke tears and hysteria in his mother, he asked to speak with Ellen, his sixteen-year-old sister. He was unaware that she had been receiving unwanted attention from a man, and that Mindy had been instructed to summon a parent to an extension line for any male caller. Perhaps because it was long distance, Mindy failed to recognize the voice on the phone as her brother's. When Ellen said hello, their mother was listening. None the wiser, Richard announced his marriage. The expression on his face said it all. His mother asked if my parents had been told, to which he stuttered, "Uh, they're sorta here." There would have been no easy way to tell them what they did not want to hear, but we were hopeful that one day they would see how deeply we loved each other and understand that we were destined to be together.

Finally it was time for my parents to leave, no longer concerned that they'd be traveling in darkness as they'd feigned on the night of my college graduation. But Fate has a sense of humor! We waved wistfully at the rear of the car as it pulled away, not realizing that the exquisite lingerie I had so lovingly selected for our wedding night was nestled cozily in the trunk, bound for home. There I was, as I would be again so many years later, without my clothes. Back upstairs we scampered about the suite, exploring each of the seven rooms. We discovered that, as it was more political camp than bridal chamber, there were only twin beds throughout! We snuggled close on a tiny mattress, and I began my life as a wife wearing my new husband's pajama tops. Richard wore the bottoms.

REFLECTIONS

I t would be a lie to say I never looked back. For years I regretted passing up medical school, but never my decision to marry Richard. I somehow thought that I could have had it all. Then, when I was forty, I met a woman who opened my eyes and finally closed the door on my discontent. The same age as I, she was single, with a doctorate from Harvard and an enviable Madison Avenue job. Visiting our home for the weekend, she watched with obvious longing our quite ordinary and average family interactions. "I am well educated, with a fabulous position," she told me, "but I would trade it all in a heartbeat for what I see here." "Carol," I replied, "I have the utmost respect and admiration for all that you have accomplished, but I would not change my life for yours. That sheepskin and plush office cannot replace strong arms around you when you are hurting; a hand to hold when you need a little help; or the knowledge that someone thinks that you are the most important person in the world—not because you are producing, but simply because you *are*."

Before he died in 1988, from injuries sustained in a car accident, my father hovered for a month between the physical and spiritual worlds— unable to rest in peace. I now know it was because he had one more job to do and wanted to make sure I was listening. As he transitioned from the earthly to the heavenly realms, I spent many hours at University of Maryland's Shock Trauma Critical Care Recovery Unit, where I formed strong bonds with the nursing staff and even attended a critical care nurses' lecture with them. That was when I noticed something I'd never considered before. These nurses brought more than technical skills to their patients. They were valued members of the health care team—participants in a collaborative effort to conquer disease, heal traumatic injuries, and make people whole again. They personified comfort, caring, and compassion on a physical and emotional level.

They were *present* for their patients in a way that doctors were not. *I wanted to do that.* I longed to be at the bedside, forging an intimacy with patients and their families. I realized something else, too: there is no human contact during surgery. The patient is covered in sterile drapes; the doctor operates through a small square window in the fabric. There's no face. Just flesh. Just worm. Just frog. I wanted to be there with my entire self—not only my brain, eyes, arms, and hands. Dad, you got it right this time. I was meant to be a nurse—*not* a "doctor-servant" holding a thermometer and bedpan in the sixties—a sophisticated, multi-dimensional nurse in the *nineties.* I became a registered nurse in acute care orthopaedics. I also dusted off my education credentials to teach Total Joint Class to patients scheduled for hip or knee replacement surgery.

Perhaps I never achieved the professional goal I set for myself so long ago. But my personal growth has been nothing short of astonishing, thanks to the wonderful man I call my husband. Richard introduced me to myself. For years, having been taught that I had no right to an opinion (which, if I dared to offer, was often laughed at or ignored), I had no personality of my own. I did not know how to act in social situations, so I learned to cope by adopting the characteristics of some girl I admired. She was usually smart, funny, and popular. The very same mannerisms and behaviors that served her so well never worked for me, though, because I was not that girl. I came across as shallow and phony. But since I took no notice of Richard initially, I made no effort to impress him. Instead of putting on a dazzling display of brains and wit, I simply *was.* As he got to know me, the *real* me, he respected my knowledge and valued my opinions. I think I began to develop as an individual when the mirror he held up to me reflected back someone attractive, interesting, and desirable. He affirmed all that was good in me, and ferreted out strengths and talents I never knew I had. From then on, at every reference point for myself, I had a partner who supported, encouraged, and validated me. At the same time, I recognized all the good in and about him of which he was totally oblivious. We evolved into strong, capable, healthy adults together.

Bolstered by Richard's confidence in me, I chased another longstanding dream: success in the world of show dogs. But my mother was still chasing me! Just a few days after we'd married, she took Richard aside and whispered, "Whatever you do, don't let Bette get a dog. You don't need one." Let? LET??? I was a married woman, and she continued to meddle; to try to run my life. We got a dog, then another . . . .

Richard indulged my passion for the show ring and we bred, trained, and exhibited champion Finnish Spitz. The national dog of Finland was virtually unknown in this country fifty years ago. For fifteen years I gave every spare moment to the effort needed to achieve American Kennel Club recognition for this rare breed. The formal presentation we made to officers and members of the Board culminated in AKC acceptance in June, 1987.

The ultimate completion of this project gave me more than a name in the dog world. It gave me self-confidence and a sense of accomplishment that I'd never known before. Through this endeavor, I learned who I was—the real me, not the one my mother had created so many years before or the ones I'd made up along the way. I remembered when I couldn't do chores like other kids; couldn't get dates or navigate comfortably in unfamiliar surroundings like other girls did. I remembered feeling invisible. Now I was somebody in my own eyes. No longer crippled by the fear that I couldn't measure up, that I wasn't good enough, I sipped cautiously at the nectar of success for the very first time. This dog thing was mine. Wholly and completely mine. I'd started it, and I'd finished it.

I expected wins; I expected success. But I had the surprise of my life when I saw the name Victor Joris on a list of dog show judges! Could it be the same man whose artful couture creations I admired and owned so many years ago? The very one who fashioned the double-breasted, navy wool blazer with gold buttons I had on for my visit to the Ice Cream Parlor with Richard on that fateful night? I emailed him. He responded: yes, it was he! After his stint as the creative force behind Cuddlecoat, he went on to Jones NY as well as its Christian Dior Sportswear line. Time melted away as I found he was part of my world again, though in such a different context. I was pleased to be able to express to him, finally, my appreciation for the exquisite designs I once wore so proudly.

With the lesson of Harvard-educated Carol in mind, and having seen juvenile delinquency in all its manifestations during my nine years in the Probation Service, I chose to remain at home and raise our daughter myself. But I had learned the hard way, from my mom, that the dark side of devoting yourself completely to your children, investing all of your time and energy in them to the exclusion of your own passions, is that you have only their reserves to draw from. When *I* became a mother, I made sure that my day would not be ruined if the curl fell out of her hair. I would not approach ecstasy if hers was the prettiest dress at the party. While I found satisfaction elsewhere with the dogs, I allowed Kira to pursue her own interests, even if they were of no interest to me. If my mom were alive today I'd ask her, "Why didn't YOU take piano lessons? Why didn't YOU become a teacher?" You can't live your dreams through your children, nor can you dream their dreams for them.

For a time, to my great delight, Kira talked about becoming a doctor. She also showed fleeting interest in my dog hobby, taking her male to his championship when she was only eight. But, unlike me, she was free to make her own choices and eventually majored in philosophy. Today, making her home in Wales with her husband, Oliver, she devotes herself to environmental issues, graphic and healing arts, and photography. She serves as Welsh Liaison to the British Ministry of Education's Department of Home Schooling. Kira has published a children's book in the UK, *Squash and Rowan*, with her own charming illustrations. She home schools her son, "Chap."

Richard and I return often to New Haven from our home in The

Berkshires to visit our favorite haunts. At the now-coed Yale, I marvel as I watch the female students—independent, confident, self assured—oblivious to the insecurities I grew up with. If my parents had ever dropped me off in the center of Freshman Commons in 1964 I'd have just sat down and bawled my eyes out, paralyzed with fear. It makes me wonder: did my parents insist on a small, Catholic girls' college so I would not only be sheltered but *feel* sheltered? The culture shock of stepping from small and conservative Springfield into a liberal university town was something they knew I was totally unprepared for. I hate to admit it, but Dad was right yet again.

When he was wrong though, Dad was very, very wrong. Had I listened to him so many years ago and left Richard, my life would have been full of regrets. I know in my heart that if I were somehow given all the stuff of my fantasies and lost Richard, I would have nothing. But you could take away all that I possess, and with him I have everything.

So what, exactly, do I have? A husband who is faithful, passionate, attentive, and totally involved in his marriage. A husband who does not walk past me without stopping for a kiss; who calls me from the office or leaves little notes just to be in touch; who looks at me with eyes filled with love; who says I am his best friend. I know, with one hundred percent certainty, that he is always there for me. He has told me that he would happily get out of bed in the middle of the night to buy me chocolate if I should get a craving. I love him enough not to ask.

We are happier together than apart, and would rather spend time with each other than with anyone else. Who ever said you don't have to be married to be a whole person? That might be true, but there's more to the story. A chess piece which is not cracked, chipped, scratched, or damaged in any other way is indeed whole. But it is not *complete* until it is part of a set. Belonging gives it purpose and meaning. Though I see myself as a whole person, Richard completes me.

As he promised my Dad so long ago, Richard also completed law school, though Dad almost blocked his graduation. Richard found himself in a class my father was teaching. One night when grading final exams Dad came thundering down the stairs, brandishing a blue book. "Is this your work?" Dad roared (students did not put their names on their tests). Breaking into a sweat, Richard took the offending book and scanned the handwriting. He exhaled a grateful "No." "Good thing," Dad muttered. And so Richard earned his "A" among many others. After completing his studies he joined the banking industry as an attorney, and continues his successful career in private law practice presently.

When I was young I anticipated a foray into the material world, to snatch up goodies like a shopping spree winner with thirty seconds left on the clock. These would include, of course, my own Jag (thanks to Richard I had one, in classic British Racing Green). A lot older now, and a bit wiser, I am able to distinguish what I want from what I need. I no longer want very much.

I have a friend who stopped going to church ages ago, but says, "I talk to God all the time." I used to do that, too, telling Him what I wanted and what I needed. Like any composer of a Christmas list for Santa, I hoped to get everything; expected to get most things; and would have been happy with a good surprise or two thrown in. Specifically, in the husband department, I ordered someone quite different from the one I got. I hate to think about what my life would be like if He'd answered that prayer!

I have learned to trust that I am watched over and cared for by the very best. Now instead of placing orders as if God were running a heavenly shoppers' network, I simply ask, "Help me to be quiet, and to listen." Then I sit back, bemused, and watch as He demonstrates once again that I in fact do not always know what is best for me. The damnedest thing is that He hasn't been wrong yet.

And so, on our thirty-fifth anniversary, we went back to say thank you to Him in a most enchanting way. In late fall of 2004 I was wasting time at Richard's office one Sunday afternoon, playing computer games while he worked. On a whim, I decided to look up the priest who'd married us. I entered his name into the search box . . . nothing. In hot pursuit now, I tried the church. Success! There was a website. To my amazement, Fr. Balducelli was still at that parish. I dashed off a quick letter, reminding him of the circumstances that brought us to his door. I offered my opinion that it was not coincidence that led us to him and asked if he would be willing to preside if we went to Delaware to renew our marriage vows.

He replied at once. "I jumped for joy," he wrote, "when I received your letter." His excitement was tempered by the realization that he would be out of the country on our wedding date. At that time ninety-one years old, he was taking a tour group to Italy that week. He would happily do it another time, or would make the church available on May 2nd with another priest if we preferred. I thought that rather strange. After all, we had pretty much picked the church out of a phone book. We were coming to see him, not the building. We made arrangements to renew our vows with him the following Saturday.

We pulled up to the church at two o'clock that afternoon, and he was waiting outside. After an emotional greeting, he invited us to go inside and sit on the chairs placed at the altar while he donned his liturgical vestments. As we approached the ornate bronze doors, I was awed once again by their beauty. They were the only feature I remembered from so long ago. Once we stepped inside, I looked around as if seeing the church for the first time. Completely focused on Richard the first time I walked down that aisle, I had failed to look left or right and missed the glorious art and architecture now apparent throughout the building.

This exquisite example of the Romanesque style, a near-replica of the Church of San Zeno Maggiore in Verona, was such a grand dream that the Italian immigrants of Wilmington in the 1920s had nowhere near the funds to realize it. What they did have, though, were master craftsmen skills, artistic talent, flaming desire, and dogged determination. They also had Fr. Roberto Balducelli, who led the construction and was involved in every detail of its progress. No wonder he was so eager to offer the church for our return visit to St. Anthony's! The magnificent edifice is celebrated in Cari DeSantis' book, *A Labor of Love*.

I walked up that long aisle again, now with Richard by my side. We took our time and studied our surroundings appreciatively. Then Fr. Roberto appeared with two altar servers, came around to stand before us, and began to speak. He talked to us about the wonders of love and marriage, reinforcing what we already knew so well. After reading a few prayers from the little red book used for wedding ceremonies, he left it open at the front of the altar and took his position behind it to begin the Mass. Except for the father of one of the boys, there was no one else in the church. When Fr. Roberto had concluded our private service, he retreated to a side room to divest himself of his robes. We had invited him to dinner, and he would meet us at the car.

Compassionate reader that you are, you must be relieved that, finally, something went right for us. *But things do not go right for us!* Stunned, we sat like statues on those chairs, staring blankly at each other. We had not renewed our vows. I expect that, when the priest put his red book down, he intended to return to it at some later time to do the vows (at weddings they are customarily recited toward the end of the Mass). But he did not. We whispered to each other. *Should we say something? Should we just leave?* We had traveled hundreds of miles to recommit ourselves to our marriage. We hadn't done it. Richard left it up to me to decide what to do. "I can't bear to embarrass Fr. Roberto," I said. "We did have our anniversary Mass with him," he replied. "Not the same thing," I insisted. Oh well . . . we just laughed it off as another it-could-only-happen-to-us adventure; another story to tell when we returned home. As we stepped off the altar to make our exit, Richard turned to me. "Do you marry me?" he asked. "Yes!" I enthusiastically replied. "Do you marry me?" He answered a resounding "Yes!" Satisfied that our vows were renewed before God if not the priest, and after a soulful kiss, we walked back down the aisle and into the sunshine. Our fairy tale had come full circle.

I know it will never end. At dinner, we recounted for Fr. Roberto all the obstacles we had overcome to be together, especially the resistance from our families. The dear priest stared for a moment at his plate. Then with shining eyes he looked up at Richard, and at me. Commanding our rapt attention with his penetrating gaze, he dismissed all those factors which loomed large in our lives so long ago. This gentle, saintly man of great wisdom condensed the secret, the success, the wonder of our life together into one sweet, simple truth.

"Above all else," he said, "there is love."

About the Author

Bette Isacoff taught high school English after college, and has been a juvenile probation officer and computer programmer. She is also a registered nurse.

Bette bred, trained, and exhibited Champion, Group, and Best in Specialty Show winning Finnish Spitz under the Kitsuna (reg.) prefix. She is credited with bringing the breed from total obscurity in this country to recognition by the American Kennel Club.

Her writing has appeared in the American Kennel Club *GAZETTE*, *Dog Fancy*, *Golden Ages Magazine*, and *The National Observer*. She was the creator and 20 year editor of *The Finnish Line* (monthly newsletter of the Finnish Spitz Club of America), and is a professional member of the Dog Writers Association of America.

Isacoff obtained her BA, and MFA in Creative Writing, from Albertus Magnus College. She is currently developing a Writing for the Web course for the Computer Information Systems Program at Albertus. She resides in The Berkshires with her husband, Richard, and their two protection-trained German Shepherd Dogs.

www.betteisacoff.com
headwindspublishing.com